Creature Comforts: My Lifelong Evolution From A($$hØ!e) To Z(achary) - Part 1

Creature Comforts: My Evolution From A($$ho!e) To Z(achary)

Zachary Perelman

Published by Zachary Perelman, 2024.

CREATURE COMFORTS: MY LIFELONG EVOLUTION FROM A($$HØ!E) TO Z(ACHARY) - PART 1

First edition. March 14, 2024.

ISBN: 979-8224694006

Written by Zachary Perelman.

Table of Contents

Dedication and Introduction

First, thank you, the reader, for taking time from your finite existence to read my memoirs. We all have a story. That you are making an effort to read these words lends credence to the story of my lifelong campaign for personal self-worth. If someone discovers one fragment of guidance via the trials and errors of my personal and professional struggles, this literary pursuit will have been well worth the elbow grease. Riffing from one of my favorite quotes, that of Sir Isaac Newton, "If I have seen further than others, it is by standing upon the shoulders of giants." I am certainly no giant, though I've had the privilege of standing upon the shoulders of a few along the way. The following memoir is my best attempt to make tribute to the wisdom of those titanesque guardians of virtue.

Secondly, I offer the most heartfelt apologies to every last individual of my past I may have directly or indirectly slighted or transgressed against. The past few years– or months, more specifically– have been unimaginably humbling in countless ways. Every last aspect of my personal, professional, intellectual, and emotional self-development has been questioned, prodded, and challenged beyond any measure I would wish upon anyone else. By this divinely orchestrated collage of adversity, I can only proclaim myself to be a more complete individual. Discomfort, in all of its iterations, has its peculiar power to equalize the imbalances of nature via the law of humility. My effort to dismantle the cultivated ego of my teens through my thirties has been a concerted one of the proverbial flow of "two steps forward and one step back." Even so, it's a long overdue pursuit and one to which I feel obliged to commit myself until my body becomes fertilizer for the flowers. Because of these circumstances, I now believe myself savvy enough to recant my past through a lens of constructive criticism without being so morally stringent as to live within a constant shadow of shame and regret– a customarily self-destructive tendency of mine.

It should be noted that the names of people, businesses, and other identifying details have been altered to preserve everyone's privacy. A few other creative liberties have been taken for literary flow. That being said, everything detailed reflects my most accurate recollections. Though some superficial facts have been modified for the aforementioned purposes, the essential details of each essay are as factual as the human memory will allow.

Lastly, this book is dedicated to my mother, father, siblings, grandparents, extended family, dearest friends, everyday acquaintances, professional associates, civil servants, unsung heroes, blue-collar workers, overlooked do-gooders, and everyone else chopping the wood in forging honorable lives for themselves. Not only would I not have logistically made it this far without your continued inspiration and practical support, but I would've quit believing in myself and the world at large without you. The existentialist's life has been anything but effortless, yet you all are the ones who make it worth living. For this, I am forever in your debt. May the impact of this endeavor sufficiently and eternally honor the invaluable legacies you have imbued upon me.

May we all have the courage to move forward each day...

-ZP

Section 86*

<u>86 or eighty-six (/ādē'siks/)</u> - American slang used to indicate that an item is no longer in stock, traditionally from a food or drinks establishment, or referring to a person or people who are not welcome on the premises

Who would've known that Sunday night in May of 2013 would be the final evening I would find myself a full-time, fine-dining server trudging through the motions at the Section 37 wine bar and bistro in the downtown Denver theater district?

I had been a server for the better part of the eight years out of college, and frankly, when I was in the flow, I was damn fine at it. I had a nearly perfect confluence of charm, social skills, and multi-tasking abilities, and all paired with my neurotic sense of urgency. That same intrinsic and driving feeling that dominated my twenties and most of my thirties– that something of an existential nature was going highly unfulfilled– somehow also doubled to make sure my orders to the kitchen and bar were sharp and that my offerings were delivered as expediently as any other server in-house. But in general, I was subconsciously done. I was hen-pecked. I hated that my philosophy education had ultimately rendered me this– a glorified servant. I didn't know it then, but I was also about to walk into a buzzsaw that night.

The fun thing about Section 37 is that it was consistently a complete and utter dumpster fire. Born of the ambition to be *the* posh wine bar at the bottom of the luxury-living Centennial Building and featuring the delicacies of an arrogant 25-year-old brat of a culinary arts graduate, it was an entity that could never seem to get out of its own way. The "managing" owner was absentee at best. In all reality, it was an open secret that he was partying the profits of the business away behind the scenes, following his favorite band around the world like some sort of trust funder Deadhead. He was a ghost.

The kitchen was run with this sense that Big Brother was always watching. The chef was an insecure tyrant and paranoid that people might be enjoying themselves in his absence. The GM, Brett, was a total jabroni, a cartoon rendition of some New York wise guy wannabe. Imagine Chachi, minus Joanie, and any semblance of a personality. He never had on less than $1k worth of clothes, always had a pomade-greased head reminiscent of Danny Zuko– and which he constantly checked in the mirror– and this low, tough-guy, unwaveringly monotone voice that could make you bite your lip bloody to keep from laughing to his face. It was as if he was straight out of central casting, and we all were permanently on *Candid Camera*. We all called him "Jersey Shore" when he wasn't around.

And the running joke of the restaurant is that we were always "86" this, that, or the other. It didn't matter if it was orange juice, Johnny Walker Black, french fries, the special I just happened to sell all of my tables, or any given dozen of the 40 bottles on the house wine list; there was forever this day-late-and-dollar-short pretext to the place. It was an organization that couldn't even settle a dispute on salt and pepper shakers for good God. Should they go on the tables or be presented upon request? Do we like our current porcelain ones– even though they constantly break– or should we upgrade to something better? If we upgrade to something better, what's the threshold of being too nice so that people don't start stealing them? The intricacy of the idiocy, incompetence, and negligence of leadership knew no end.

Oh yes. It was on that night when the time-honored "camel's back" was broken.

You see, Sunday nights down on 14th and California used to be a very hit-and-miss prospect of an evening. It always depended on what was or wasn't going on between the convention center and the adjacent performance theaters. That night was anticipated to be about as dead as possible by every indication. No conventions were in town. *Wicked* was long gone– just some stale reruns on the theater scene. Very few reservations were on the books. Everything seemed rather status quo, so true to the form of trying to squeeze a penny, Brett cut the hostess, busser, and one of us three servers. I had the option to be the one to get cut for the night. I declined– a fateful decision.

It should also be mentioned that we were short two line cooks that night. I couldn't tell you why. One probably was too hungover to make it and called in with something "contagious." I can only imagine the other joined the legions before him and decided he had enough of keeping Mussolini's trains running on time. At any rate, it was the boniest of skeleton crews I had ever worked with at that place– a sous chef and two middling line cooks.

Add to this brotherhood of achievers Brett and the Diana Ross diva "Mixologist," Kendall. If you insisted on calling him a bartender past his first correction of you, he just might surreptitiously spit in your Blackberry Mint Negroni. Kendall wasn't the worst cat I'd ever worked with, but he was incredibly vain and practically useless when you found yourself in a pinch. The kitchen crew furtively referred to him as "Guyliner" or "Manscara" due to his conspicuous religiosity of doting over his eye makeup more than his professional duties.

What to do with Sazerac, Absinthe, simple syrup, and a muddle of citrus? There's your guy. Need a warm beer poured and ready within 15 minutes during a mild dinner rush? Not on his firstborn's life. My long-deceased grandmother could fire off drinks faster than that joker.

This was my team. We were the 14th Street *Bad News Bears.*

The first hour or two of dinner service was going fine. We had a walk-in or two. Well over half of our reservations were in the process of eating or were already happily on their way home. The pork tenderloin was coming out perfectly medium-rare. The Brussels sprouts delivered their usual crunchy goodness. What few glasses of wine I was asked to retrieve actually were where I needed them to be. And fortuitously enough, no one had gotten froggy and done something *insanely* labor-intensive and positively unprofitable– ordering a setup of hot herbal tea replete with lemon, honey, stevia, and my best impression of trying not to lament you to your face. Things looked like they might even be downright easy there for a second. And then, the dam broke. It broke in cinematic fashion.

Now, this was a restaurant that could seat over 80 patrons at any given time. Based on the roster mentioned above, I would say that we maybe could give lights-out service to a small handful, good service to maybe ten, and sufficient service to absolutely no more than 15 or 16. At some point around that 6:30 or 7:00 hour, the walk-ins began. Two here. Four there. A couple of singles tested their fate at the bar with Diana Ross.

Before I knew it, my prolonged and polished opening spiel– including the cocktail and dinner specials, and embedded with a few corny jokes– rapidly became a "Hey there. I got some water here for ya. I'll return in ten to take all the drink and food orders simultaneously, so please be ready. My apologies for the crazy nature of all of this. We might have misscheduled our labor resources this evening". And for a brief while, say 20 minutes or so, this frenetic pace of greet, seat, welcome, and accommodate was somehow working. Sure, the patrons weren't getting their usual white-glove service, but naturally, they could see that we were hustling to no end, truly making lemonade out of that ever-mounding pile of lemons. Something had to give. Indeed, this had all the makings and nervous energy to go into a total nuclear meltdown.

The monkey wrench heaved into the heart of the gear works was quite the catalyst for the show. As I was at the screen of the computer at the server station– breathing somewhat heavily and sweating profusely thanks to the non-stop sprint from front door to table, table to kitchen, kitchen to bar, bar back to table, etc.– the screen went into the "spinning wheel of death" as I've heard some refer to it. You know, that unending spin of a circle set dead center on any given computer screen– it spun, and it spun, and it spun. Before I could hypothetically put my fist through it at this moment of sheer operational chaos, the screen went totally black. She went black for a good two or three hours.

Enter Defcon 1.

At this point, we must have had up to about 20 people in-house and another two or three groups standing at the hostess stand, seemingly in sheer disbelief as to what was devolving in front of their eyes. Food orders placed an hour before sat untouched in the kitchen window for 15-20 minutes at a time. The cocktails ordered concurrently sat immaculately still at the bar, the ice melted out, wallowing in pools of condensation. Tables of satiated patrons, surrounded by empty water glasses and sullied plates, waited with supernatural, monk-like patience. Spills of this. Messes of that. I'm pretty sure one of the line cooks even stepped out for a smoke right as we hit the full crescendo of madness.

Now, a competently run establishment would have had on hand what is commonly known in the restaurant industry as a "crash kit." It's that ancient apparatus from the deepest annals of my memory of the '80s– the ubiquitous, antiquated slab with the floating mechanism that flows over and back one's credit card, leaving the card's impression upon the carbon copy paper beneath. Well, guess what...86 the crash kit. I can't imagine one ever existed in this abomination in the first place.

This reality resulted in the imminent walk-of-shame around to my handful of tables. This walk primarily consisted of a proclamation of embarrassment followed by an explanation regarding the nature of the night's horrors. With all of this also came the admission that due to the nature of the restaurant's infrastructural shortcomings, they were legally free to walk out on their open tab and that I wouldn't blame them one iota if they chose that route. As I recall, one table was happy to spitball it and cover their estimated tab with a wad of cash, which I ultimately made to include a 30% gratuity for myself at night's end. Another table said they only had a credit card to cover anything close to what should have been their tab. They threw me $20 from their wallet, thanked me for what little service I *could* provide them, and wished me Godspeed. One group told me they didn't have a lick of hard currency on them. It might as well have been an *Oliver Twist* situation– Victorian England orphan standing in front of me, palms up, pockets inside out, and a look upon their bewildered faces as unpromising as a tips-based laborer could hope for. Off they walked– not a dime on the table.

Sometime just before or just after that shameful walk, I recall having turned to the collection of people still languishing at the vacated hostess stand– about a dozen or so– and said something along these lines: "Folks, I'm not sure what to say to you all other than I admire your patience incredibly and would encourage all of you to do right by yourselves, walk out our front door, make a right, and walk about six blocks until you get to Larimer Street. You'll know it's Larimer because the entire street for the length of the city block will be covered in strings of festive lights. Pick literally *any* food establishment on that street, and your dining experience will be one thousand times better than anything I can *possibly* offer you this evening. This place is a cruel joke. I encourage you all to get on Yelp or Open Table and leave the most scathing and detailed review of what you've witnessed here as you're willing to. I'm beyond embarrassed to be the one here telling you fine folks all of this. And honestly, I'm fairly certain this will be the last night I ever work at this dog and pony show. My sincerest regrets."

My soliloquy did its job. That spurned group of patrons applauded my candor and attitude. Much like most of my empathetic tables that night, they wished me far better of an evening than I had experienced to that point, and out the door and off to bona fide dining experiences they went. Thank you, God.

After what seemed like an eternity but was probably more like three hours, the palpable buzz of the calamity progressively began to ease into more of a rehab period. Cold food was delivered. A few drinks were remade and presented in reasonable time. Everything was effectively free for the patrons for the rest of the night, no questions asked. Given the computer situation, I even made a couple of bucks despite some nullified transactions and my lack of logistical ability to drive sales. The tide was slowly starting to turn, but the damage was done. I was starving. I had a full bladder, which I'd been holding onto for hours. My gas tank far exceeded "E." The restaurant was an unprecedented mess. Patrons were systemically disappointed. But it was all about to be over. That was until...

"Sir," squeaks the weiner with the nasally-pitched voice from my last, lingering, and unforgivingly annoying table, "where are the salt and pepper shakers?"

That was it. Those ten syllables sealed the deal. I was done. The albatross of Section 37— calamity embodied as dysfunctional, perpetually clogged, terminally broken, frequently absent, porcelain, salt and pepper shakers— would obliterate what tolerance I had left for this godawful abortion of a job. The question would freeze me in my tracks. For a full second, maybe two, I just stood frozen, staring in the middle distance, and an audible chuckle overtook me. Just like that, I realized that I was free. It could be over as soon as I hit the John, clocked out, and dreamed up that next chapter of my life. Where was I going? What exactly was next? I wasn't sure. All I knew was that this professional existence had become fundamentally unlivable, and certainly, there must've been better ways for me to live out my terrestrial days.

Being the stalwart human and professional that I am, I acquiesced to the request, delayed my bodily relief even another few seconds, and retrieved those evasive and abysmal shakers for what would turn out to be the last table I would ever administer as a full-time server. I mean, at this juncture– my having forever absolved myself after this slapstick evening of this unending punishment of a career– why not? It would be a profound pleasure to see any requested task through now that the writing was on the wall. And onto the table I placed the requested shakers. Of course, I didn't receive a thank you or any form of acknowledgment, but whatever. I was done making elaborate, sweeping moral judgments based on the small-minded practices of hangry, everyday grumps like this putz.

Let them finish, present their check– once again possible with the computer system finally restored hours later– and see them out. That was it. That would be the very end of this dystopian existence of mine. As I turned and walked away, "Sir," the voice of my last snowflake pierced the serenity of the aftermath, "do you have any hot herbal tea, by chance?"

Craptown Races

Growing up a midwestern Jew, there was a phenomenon to which I was once subjected– Jew Camp. For whatever reason, Jewish kids growing up were, and seemingly have been for generations, not only encouraged to go off to sleepaway camp during the summer but, moreover, were tribally conscripted to do as much. I know how that must read on paper in the year 2024, but this is in no way some sort of self-deprecating schtick or morbid association with the Holocaust. Indeed, sleepaway summer camp among my Jewish brethren has been a prominent focus for decades. I imagine it was born of the idea of establishing a highly intimate sense of cultural identity amongst young Jews so that we could grow up and proliferate our ancient culture, comprised of a relatively minuscule number of members. Perhaps it was just a collectively intelligent way to exile masses of children from the house for a couple of weeks, facilitating large-scale, communal respite of uninterrupted marital relations (Yuck). Most likely, it was both.

I'm sure other religions and cultures have fostered similar ideals and practices for their young. Still, I have a hard time believing that many, if any, of them are quite as adamant about their youth taking to the summer camp experience as we Jews. Most of my peers took to summer camp as though it was some sort of substitute for a full year of Hebrew school or, better yet, having to sit in synagogue *ever* again. Not for me. I *hated* summer camp. And once upon a time, in the summer of 1991, I was thrust into embarking upon that sacred, ancestral birthright.

Well before that summer, sandwiched between my second and third grade of schooling, the conditioning for overnight camp had begun. Around late preschool or kindergarten, it was commonplace for my friends and me to go to day camp for a large portion of the summer. Each summer was divided into three sessions, and I was typically enrolled in at least two, if not all three. From Monday through Friday, we would spend the hours of the day generally reserved for school, enjoying the boundless offerings of unscripted youthful fun.

We constantly played the crowd-favorite *War Ball*– dodgeball on a full-sized basketball court, with the end goal being to sink a half-court shot on the other team's basket to win. We swam twice every day. We ate lunches packed by our moms and loaded with some of the best-tasting, most ultra-processed junk food in the history of American gluttony. We laughed. We told dirty jokes. We jostled and tormented each other, as social gatherings of young boys inevitably tend to do.

It was awesome!

The days were packed with non-stop fun and games, and then around 4 P.M., your mom would come to pick you up, and you could go home and spend the rest of the day watching cable from an air-conditioned couch or riding bikes around the neighborhood or doing absolutely nothing at all. What a concept! It was the best of all worlds. Not only could I have all of that fun at camp all day, but I could also play Little League at night or on the weekends, eat home cooking, dump in my own toilet, and sleep in my own bed every night. It was a perfect balance of activity, inertia, and creature comforts, but apparently, it wasn't a script to be followed once younger children developed into older children.

Yes, the common belief must be that once a child has crossed the threshold of age ten or so, they are ready to go from part-time to full-time camper. I would have to say that seemingly, the whole group of us was prepared to cross this rubicon except for one– me. I had no idea of knowing it at the time, but somewhere along the way, I had become such a momma's boy and homebody in those early years that the idea of staying away from home for any prolonged period of time was indeed a crippling notion. Sure, once or twice, when I started sleeping over at friends' houses, I recall insisting on going home to sleep in my bed. But that was relatively common for five, six, or seven-year-olds. By the time I was nine, I still had yet to shake that separation anxiety, and the effects were immediate. Additionally, as previously hinted upon, my inner 80-year-old Jewish princess– which has apparently resided deep within since the beginning– was decidedly not into defecating in public bathrooms. Having to step in the "batter's box while playing a road game" has not only been a historically reviled proposition but also something that my subconscious psyche would oftentimes render a physiological impossibility.

It stands to reason that my memory of that single attempt at sleepaway camp would remain one of my more vivid recollections of childhood memory. Trauma has an uncanny penchant for permanently impressing itself upon the human memory, whether real or perceived. In retrospect, I would have to qualify my "traumatic" sleepaway summer camp experience as perceived, not real trauma. Nobody forced me to go. Nobody hurt or neglected me. I was continuously surrounded by countless characters I considered my best friends. The counselors were friendly and fun. The older kids were cool to me, seeing as my siblings were well respected within their respective social circles. Activities abounded. The food wasn't great, but it wasn't awful either, and true to '90s form, we were given multiple full-sized chocolate bars each day. Hell, it was only a mere two-week session. I had zero reason to hate my situation, but hate it, I did. In fact, within an hour or so of arriving the very first day at the rustic shack of our cabin, I waited for all the other guys to get settled and go out to mess around our new environment so I could sob myself silly into the haven of my packed pillow, which still very much smelt like home.

I'm reasonably certain my efforts to mask my homesickness were feeble at best. By the second day, all my friends knew they loved camp and that I just wanted to go home and be surrounded by familiarity. We weren't allowed to call home over those two weeks, but we were allowed to send letters via the old Pony Express. My mom had sent me off with a bunch of envelopes, stamps, and a stack of blank forms to fill out with pre-selected topics for me to fill in. It was a questionnaire to get little boys to write more than two sentences when checking in with their parents. Prompts read like: "Today at camp we had the best time____________," or "My favorite activity at camp is ________________."

Instead of filling out the well-purposed, pre-fab letters the way they were intended, I used the opportunity to write one singular sentence for each letter to be sent. Rather than filling in the blank of one or two or all of the prompts, I would simply write in massive letters– down the length of the paper, spanning the space of multiple prompts– "This place fucking blows."

Even though I was by far the youngest of three children in a liberal household and lived the most unsheltered existence of all of my peers as a result, I wasn't exactly allowed to cuss openly at that age. By age eight, I had seen every Jon Hughes teen raunch-com at least five times, and I knew *Revenge of the Nerds* by heart– especially when the nudie scenes were coming up. In this regard, I was a PhD among my peers. And sure, my parents never got bent out of shape if I did get caught slipping here or there, but they were far too respectable to allow their second grader to spout off like some sort of stereotype of a truck driver.

I didn't care. As I saw it, maybe if I kept it profane and stark enough– one sentence per mailed letter– then just perhaps, they might take a hint and drive short of two hours from Omaha to wherever in God's name Milford, Nebraska is to pick up their brooding little brat. I made a point of sending out a solid handful of those thinly veiled S.O.S. notes in the first few days. Despite my best attempts, the letters were responded to with care packages and letters of support and encouragement to see the whole two weeks through. The pissy little Sylvia Plath camper I had become was nonplussed with their decision not to indulge my short-sighted and pampered wishes. It was great parenting on their part.

Shortly after we arrived, two of my parents' dearest friends, Patty and Steve Nogg, who at that time were chairpeople for the camp sponsor of the Jewish Federation, arrived unannounced to check up and see how everything was going in Milford. When I saw them, for a fleeting moment, I thought my prayers had been answered. Patty and Steve loved me, and I loved them. Indeed, if my idiot parents weren't catching my drift via my begrudging correspondences, the Noggs would save me. As I recall, I made a point to slip away from my group and approach them straight away. I don't precisely remember my pitch, but I definitively remember that when my words failed to convey my dire need to escape summer camp, I resorted to attempted bribery. As she recalls thirty-some years later, I covertly whispered under my breath, "Hey Patty, I'll give ya five bucks if you'll take me home."

For the price of five whole American dollars, I would be willing to purchase my freedom. All they had to do was smuggle me in their backseat as they left camp and drop me off at home once they got back to Omaha. One Abraham Lincoln could've been theirs, no questions asked. It was no small chunk of cash, but I was willing to part with it to get back to my comfort zone. I didn't know it then, but our dear friends Patty and Steve didn't need $5, nor were they going to let me off the hook where my parents forced me to stay. Instead of accepting my offer, they laughed hysterically at the proposition. True to their wholesome character, they offered the same infuriating positivity and encouragement my parents did and left me to wallow. Bless them.

After the first week, which felt more like three months, my pervading feeling of homesickness mysteriously began to fade. Rather than looking for any and every excuse to go back to lying in my cabin bed during the day, I actually started to enjoy myself. The food was getting better. Pickup games of kickball weren't all bad. The talent show was mildly entertaining. Throwing shit at the girls as they participated in arts and crafts was timelessly gratifying. In fact, archery was downright fun. Maybe this overnight camp wasn't the worst of things after all. But I still hadn't pooped. Whatever. Dietary fiber intake wasn't precisely my overriding preoccupation, especially when faced with the proposition of frequenting the open-air, spider-infested commodes.

Ironically, the most fun I had during those two weeks was participating in a game, the theme of which has aged horribly in today's lens of political correctness. It was called *Escape From Russia*. It was effectively a late-night version of a campus-wide rendition of *Tag*. Most campers were grouped into "Jewish families" and dispersed among various cabins and buildings on one side of the campus. The counselors —and maybe some older kids, I can't wholly recall— would dress up in garb, which I guess was somewhat to resemble a Cossack or Soviet or whichever oppressor du jour, and they would patrol the center of camp, role-playing as though they had Jews to catch and imprison, which they inevitably did— in the infirmary. As a family unit, we aimed to sneak from our side of camp, across the gauntlet of Commies, and over to the far side of camp, where The Red Enemy could no longer persecute us. We were outfitted with phony passports, fictitious backstories, and a warning that our prospects of escaping Russia were exceedingly grim.

I couldn't even begin to tell you exactly how the game unfolded that evening. I can only tell you that a bunch of young Jews ran around playing a glorified game of hide-and-seek that night, and we loved it. I believe the whole intention was for us to appreciate better the harrowing journeys our forebearers had made for their descendants to build better lives in the New World. Instead, we had ourselves a good old-fashioned run around the yard. Nothing was taught. No wisdom was gained. Discussing cultural persecution and New World horizons wasn't even an afterthought regarding the subject matter. Nope. But, a few kids cried from the full-contact process of being accosted by Communists and physically dragged back to the infirmary. One of the counselors fell down in pursuit of a camper and severely bruised her tailbone. Yes. The year 1991 was still an era when the term "tone-deaf" was strictly used in reference to a musical malady, and everything was more or less acceptable if it ended with a punchline befitting a Mel Brooks movie. And "liability" was hardly a term associated with the rough-and-tumble way we used to play as kids. I can only imagine someone floating the idea of playing *Escape From Russia* at a Jewish summer camp today. The outrage would cause rolling blackouts through social media– a mockumentary ripe for the making.

It finally arrived, the last day of camp. What began with the feeling of starting a lifetime sentence at San Quentin somehow was already over. I simply had to pack up my stinking heap of dirty clothes and toiletries and go to the canteen for our final breakfast before the buses would take us back to Omaha. As I eagerly shoved the mass of possessions into my duffel bag, the moment's focus instantaneously shifted. Perhaps as a result of emotional elation or, more likely, because there is only so much cubic space in a person's digestive tract, my euphoria turned to horror when I spontaneously realized today was the day to shit.

Not only did I have to take my first dump of camp on the very last day (14), but I had yet to make a plan as to what I would do if I *were* to be presented with such a scenario. When you've got to go, you've got to go. It was no longer a preference for comforts or cleanliness. No. Now, it was a sheer matter of physics. I had eaten approximately 42 meals since I left my house, and the stand of restrooms was a good three or four hundred yards down the hill, across the bridge, up another hill, and a slalom between a few cabins.

Well, the good news is that I ultimately made it. I dropped my duffel bag as though it was in flames, and somehow, I managed to shuffle my way across camp to the nearest bathroom stall slowly but steadily. For all I remember, it might have even transpired in the girls' room. I simply recall getting the stall door shut behind me, dropping trow, turning around, and painting the stall's separating wall, roll of toilet paper, back wall, a swathe of the floor, entire toilet– seat, handle, and everything but the inside of the bowl– with two weeks' worth of angst. I didn't even bother sitting down. It was over as quickly as it began.

The term "photo finish" is one I've heard used in reference to horse racing. In the same spirit of this notion, I would go ahead and say that if the objective of this particular race was to not besmirch my clothing and social standing with an explosion of feces, then I just barely "won" in a "photo finish." It's of great fortune that this is just a euphemism and was not an actual photographic undertaking. It was a scene that unequivocally needed no visual documentation. No camera should ever suffer such a fate, no matter how inanimate it might happen to be.

To this moment, I pity the unfortunate, waged employee whose job was to address that situation after the fact. It was nothing a suitable garden hose, hazmat suit, rubber gloves, nose plug, and a bracing shot of whiskey couldn't fix. However, I still feel terrible for whatever trauma was inevitably suffered at the behest of my second-grade poop neuroses. It was not my proudest moment by any means, but at least I didn't get any on me for my long bus ride home. My undies and reputation remained intact. Camp was officially over– V-Day, as I saw it.

Somehow, I made it the whole two weeks, and I was surprisingly even a little sad to be going home. Nonetheless, there was no way on God's green earth that I would ever be talked into attending sleepaway camp again, and I most certainly never did. Of course, that put me in the minority. Not only did the rest of my Jewish friends embrace the cultural expectation, they loved it. For years after that, they would travel to Wisconsin, Minnesota, Missouri, and other more distant locales to live out two-month sessions of that nonsense. I never quite understood the draw. It wasn't until I left for college at age 19 that the overriding need to reside in my static comfort zone would give in to the realities of having someday to grow up and leave my safe, coddled surroundings.

In all honesty, I'm not entirely sure what this particular narrative of my youth denotes of me other than the fact that I've been a sucker for creature comforts as long as I can remember. I'm sure, to some degree, all of us have wrestled with this monster. Yet, for whatever reason, this universal predicament has seemingly been the underlying cause for so many of my personal shortcomings over the years. It's a terminal and seemingly unsolvable paradox. Get too comfortable, and the intrinsic value of the struggle is lost. The push to become more, the drive to overcome the unpleasantness, these self-actualizing responses to adversity are rendered futile.

Or, on the other hand, suffer too much and risk losing appreciation for the struggle and its resultant growth altogether. Allow the adversity to define you, and live a life simply to spite the struggle. Live as a negative, negating the undesirable. This disposition undermines the pursuit of living life simply because life is worth living despite its unyielding and countless challenges– a supposition many will inevitably challenge. Yet what else is there? What else can we do but wrestle and vacillate back and forth between the sloth of comfort versus the masochism of constantly challenging our inherently imperfect human tendencies?

Much like most matters within the universal world of relativity in which we find ourselves, the answer lies somewhere in the middle. And the answer is, to some degree, always in flux. As humans, we seek predictability, reliability, and permanence in a world that manifestly is not designed to promote any of those ideals. We innately seek immutable algorithms by which to live our lives. Simply plug a variable into any given formula, and out the other side emerges the intended outcome, a thousand times out of a thousand. This natural and subconscious yearning for perfect order is perhaps our biggest weakness. If there is a true accomplishment to be made by any one of us perfectly imperfect creatures, it would be to recognize this unfulfilled need, address it as the stuff of fantasy, and challenge ourselves to be okay with living in the continual motion of pendulating back and forth, as we so often seem to do with such matters. In a way, it's as though we are constantly trying to establish our "sea legs" on the tumultuous ocean voyage of excess versus deficiency.

Though the years have long passed, the lesson has very much remained the same. Learn not just to be content living within the ceaselessly unknown and relatively uncomfortable but to really love it for all it is. It has repeatedly propelled me further along my path of personal development, this enduring and confounding concept of an undetermined outcome to everything. As I like to phrase it, "Learn to lean into the 'suck' of life." It's that very sobering reality that there is no finish line to any of this until we are dead and gone, which gives us a dichotomous feeling of "Good God, how much longer??" opposing "There is only a finite amount of time here, and who knows when it all ends??" If I ever accomplish anything of noteworthy merit in this lifetime, I must credit this infinite sense of unease for keeping me honest and directed. Heaven knows that as the years have passed, I've had to overcome far more than a mere two-week camping debacle as a youth. More to the point, these trials have proven to be the building blocks for the individual I am finally proud to profess that I am on my way to becoming in full.

That said, as the imperfect being that I will forever be, if I never have to "pinch hit" away from my home bowl again for the rest of a 200-year-long life, I'm fairly assured I'm willing to concede that aspect in fully becoming my best version of me. Call me a princess if you must.

Jew's On First

Very few phases of my life were as wholesome and thoroughly enjoyable as my days in Suburban Little League. Much like the name would imply, it was your rank-and-file All-American youth baseball organization smack dab in the middle of the West Omaha suburbs. It was of the traditional nature that you enlist your kid; he gets divvied up among a bunch of other kids from his and adjacent schools, and everyone actively plays on any given team named after an MLB organization. Much like any given cross-section of randomized humanity, Suburban ran the traditional bell curve of talent spanning the spectrum from too-good-to-be-in-this-league to I-hope-he-someday-finds-a-career-in-the-arts range of skill sets. I am proud to say that I was about a seven or eight on the universal ten-scale because the previous scale I mentioned is nonsense.

Don't get me wrong. I was nothing to write home about. The nines and tens were too good for the league, and after the first year, most of them went off to play for selective travel teams, the likes of which spent their summers playing 80-100+ games. Even if I had the talent for those squads, which I didn't, there's no way I would have ever pissed away a whole summer playing sports. I simply never had the dedication. The good thing with Suburban was that we never played past late June or early July, so summers were still summer. Plus, when the legitimate talent left the building, I suddenly became a top-shelf prospect.

As someone who has had an unconditioned dad bod since the third grade– minus a few years in my late twenties– I was naturally slow around the base path. Plus, my noodly arm strength and the resultant inability to whip the ball across the diamond maxed out somewhere around fourth grade and hasn't improved since. That aside, I could hit the ball consistently and with considerable power.

As a creature of the left-handed persuasion, my stance in the batter's box was typically advantageous. As a result, I habitually batted in the two, three, or four spots of the batting order. But in the field, the left-handed throw from my linguini arm and my running-through-mashed-potatoes speed made me a perfect candidate for first base. I had a vacuum for a glove, and despite my not being limber, I always made a respectable stretch to catch throw-outs. Also, my favorite player growing up was first baseman Frank Thomas of the Chicago White Sox. He was about 6'5", 275lbs., black, and a bearer for the reputation of swinging a hammer for a bat and circling the bases in slow motion. With my newfound defensive identity, it was obvious that he and I were essentially twins.

Sentimentally speaking, I will always hold a special place in my heart for Suburban because my dad primarily coached my teams. He wasn't the head coach every season, but more often than not, he was. And if he wasn't head coach, he was a highly involved assistant coach. He never put undue pressure on me to do anything other than try my best and enjoy the fun. Even more to that point, he would frequently have to reel me in after a bad performance and insist that my Little League batting average would never move the needle on any loan application or job interview of my adult future. I didn't care what he said. I kept my stats anyhow. I was pretty liberal, gifting myself hits where others might mark fielding errors. But even so, I batted above the .500 mark annually and could routinely put the ball on a rope to the outfield. Coach's kid or not, I was annually one of the best players on my team.

The season before fifth grade fostered my most vivid memory from my summer days at Lamp Park. The complex had several differently-sized fields, and sometimes, due to scheduling conflicts, we would be relegated to fields smaller or larger than those of our intended age group. Typically, when there was a scheduling conflict, the league would try to err one size up on the fields for public safety reasons and to keep the games played within more competitive confines. We had to play on a field designed for the younger Mustang Leaguers on this particular day. We were in Bronco League, meaning our fields were roughly one hundred feet longer.

At this point in our prepubescent lives, nobody on any of my previous teams had ever hit a home run over the fence. I had heard of it happening in another game or two, but it wasn't much of a physiological possibility for most of us boys. This fateful day, on the first pitch, as the third batter in the top of the first inning, I ended that era. I sent a meatball not just over the fence but *wayyy* over the fence. It was legitimately a bomb, and I'm reasonably confident it would have been out on one of our standard-sized fields. I distinctly remember my dad serving as first base coach and seeing him impulsively jump straight up with his hands in the air in a celebration that must've felt like watching his son win the Super Bowl. His enthusiasm was contagious.

I've heard the phrase, "Act like you've been there," regarding people keeping cool and not utterly geeking out when dopamine floods the brain post-achievement. Well, I acted like the ten-year-old amateur that I very much was. I hugged my dad as I rounded first, spun circles as I passed second, and reenacted the famous 1988 Kirk Gibson World Series celebratory arm pumps as I circled third for home. It was beyond obnoxious, but it was a watershed moment in my local generation's world of sporting accomplishments. The rest of the game didn't matter. Hell, the rest of the season didn't matter. I was a big deal. I was clearly going places.

By the third inning, my buddy and teammate, Pat Werner, hit his own dinger well over dead-center. Not one inning later, the stud catcher on the other team, Brian Spreewell, hit a moonshot that looked like it went as far as mine, plus Pat's. Just like that, I was brought back to Earth. But for a good thirty minutes in fifth grade, I was thinking about putting my imminent future in medical school on hold to explore life in the MLB farm system.

My last few years playing for Suburban concluded with me participating in the league's traveling All-Star team. These teams would travel around Eastern Nebraska and Western Iowa, beginning a few weeks before the end of the regular in-house season and ending a few weeks after. Unlike the previously mentioned ultra-dedicated select teams, we weren't a finely tuned machine by any measure. But we were a solid group from top to bottom and could hold our own with most teams in the metro area.

Unlike my typical in-house squad, I was just another formidable player among a dozen others. I still played first, but I rarely started. When I did play, I was usually slotted somewhere in the six to eight range of the batting order. I quit keeping my stats as the competition got honest, and my usual games of going three for four or four for six from the plate were long gone. The competition could throw curveballs and sliders, and rarely did a hit ball whiz past any infield defenders. I was no longer a marlin in a puddle-size pond. In one respect, it wasn't nearly as fun as regular Suburban League. In addition to my losing Big Fish status, none of the guys on my team were organically friends of mine. They were alright guys, but with me sitting in the dugout way more than in the old days and no one of particular interest to screw around with when I was benched, the All-Star days didn't quite manage to hold the same nostalgic magic for me all these years later.

Of course, I had my moments of game-changing plays. One time, I made the final two outs of the game by grounding a ball hit straight to me at first, stepping on the bag to force out the batter, and throwing the ball on a dime for the catcher to tag out the greedy runner trying to force the issue at the plate. We won the game 1-0. Or another time, I hit a one-hop-to-the-fence single off of a cat who was 6'4", regularly in need of a shave, and ultimately went on to start for the University of Nebraska in college. Athletically speaking, within the world of competition, it's been a freefall ever since.

My baseball days were behind me when I hit high school. My arm never came around. I didn't bother working on my speed. The rookie years of my smoking various carcinogens were just upon me. I loved my baseball days for all they were and all they weren't, which is to say, like the one year I tried to play full-contact football. It was the fall after my legendary home run, and I figured I'd try my hand at the sport that was quickly taking over as the primary object of my sports-viewing interests. As it happened, come autumn, Lamp Park doubled as a practice ground for the storied West Omaha Wildfire franchise.

In the fall of 1993, I finally tested the waters of being a two-sport phenom, much like one of my childhood heroes, Bo Jackson. Just like Suburban in-house, making the Wildfire roster was as merit-based as having parents dutiful enough to make it up to the parking lot of Cub Foods between noon and three on some random Sunday in August and not have their checks bounce. With that formula for unmitigated success, our particular organization managed to field a roster of 14 eager young boys, each of us with designs on being the next great Chief or Cowboy.

With a roster of that few, we would inevitably have to adopt what is traditionally known as the "iron man" operation of football, meaning everyone had to play offense, defense, and special teams. Only three guys at a time could get a rest on any given play, and that was *if* everyone was healthy. Most other squads in the greater metro area fielded teams of 20 or more, so most of their guys were designated for offense *or* defense, plus minimal special teams. As any monkey with half a brain can deduce, that set us up for abject exhaustion by halftime of every game we played. As I previously touched upon in denoting my lifelong dad bod, I was no physical specimen when it came to my general physical conditioning. Nonetheless, I wasn't remotely the least conditioned guy on the team. I never did, but a few permanent linemen regularly puked multiple times per practice.

We were a godawful mess, but at least my plucky spirit and willingness not to shy away from a tackle solidified my standing as captain of the defense. Much like the divine ordination of my destiny to play first base because of my love of Frank Thomas, I was naturally destined for linebacking greatness, much like my all-time favorite NFLer, the late, great Derrick Thomas. I knew I wasn't quite as quick-twitch as my professional muse, but I would uquestionably make up for it by watching *SportsCenter* highlights every night. Whether it was one Thomas or the next, I was set to mimic sporting success at its highest echelons.

And then, the season happened. True to our namesake, we were a smoldering tire fire of epic proportions. When the soot settled, we boasted a 0-9 record, and two of our trusty 14 were lost to injury halfway through the season. The year's highlight was the 45-yard composite loss of field position thanks to our head coach, Benny. It resulted from three consecutive unsportsmanlike penalties earned in under a minute. I can't remember precisely what he said to the ref, but it most likely involved comments about the official's wife or mom. Five minutes after being ejected, Benny returned from the adjacent snack shack with a cup of coffee and shadowed the ref on the field, badgering him until security was notified. In retrospect, Benny and his esteemed band of scholarly assistant coaches, Gary and Joel, were the real story of the season. Not only did none of the three have sons on the team, but if any of them did have kids in general, it was highly improbable they were allowed to accompany them outside of court-ordered supervision.

Benny was a skinny and skeezy-looking character with a handlebar mustache who always wore aviator sunglasses and a dirty, once-white hat with "Beach Bum" scribbled across the front in a neon pink *Miami Vice* font. He might have been the prototype for Joe Dirt had he been a hyperbolic caricature of a sex offender charged with running a youth football team.

Gary was about 5'2", 330lbs, and never wore a tee shirt without the armpits soaked out. The prolonged drawl of his every sentence and his conspicuously absent incisors didn't stump well for his cause of being well-received among sheltered, middle-class youth. Gary looked eerily like the generic bad guy in the *Stranger Danger* videos we watched at school. Every breath of his sounded laborious, and he loved to yell until he was light purple in the face. His blood pressure had to have been measured in PSI; If he is still alive today, I'll eat my own head.

And then there was Joel. Joel didn't do shit. He didn't say anything. He didn't demonstrate anything. He stood around, took up space, and chain-smoked Newports. The practice field was his mosaic of cigarette butts, something resembling an Eastern Bloc prison yard, I'd have to imagine. It was almost as if his continued parole depended on our notching a "1" in the win column. Yet, with every loss, he offered nothing to the cause. If it wasn't for the battlefield of spent menthols, we might have even confused him for a recurring apparition of the guy Benny and Gary shot in their presumably bungled bank robbery.

That was the brain trust. The powers that be put those three in charge of 14 fifth graders. I thank everything holy that my dad had no business in this coaching pursuit. Of all the great mysteries of my life, the assemblage of the "coaching staff" of the 1993 West Omaha Wildfire will forever remain one of the most bewildering. There's virtually no way they voluntarily took up such roles as leaders of young men. One can only surmise that one or multiple judges met those specimens in various legal settings and figured, "What the hell? If these savants are gonna do some community service, it would probably be in everyone's best interest if they were to supervise youth participating in a notoriously violent sport. Let's get those kids coached up."

Despite my hallowed status as defensive captain, I would never again strap on football pads after that season. As much as I hated relinquishing my pursuit of multiple-sport stardom, I knew my short time in the game was over. I had to focus on more academic affairs. The girls at school were starting to get their boobies, and my youthful downtime was better spent figuring out how to endear myself to a pair of those. Plus, Jews are what we are at sports, and I was no Julian Edelman. I had mastered the art of football on Sega Genesis, and one season in Benny's program was more pigskin than I could stomach in this life. Boasting an inflated batting average as a seven at first base would do just fine. And my old man was right. My lifetime slugging percentage in Suburban hasn't impacted my credit score one way or another.

The Lamest Goth Phase You've Never Heard Of

In hindsight, growing up in Omaha was a perfect "Catch-22" for me. As they say, "Youth is wasted on the young," and it wasn't until well into my twenties that I realized how lucky I was to have been grounded in such a place during the formative years of my life. Every generality has its exceptions, of course, but the people of Omaha, and the better part of Middle America for that matter, are by and large well-intended do-gooders. The individual cultures and various demographics therein will invariably clash with this detail or that practice. Even so, once you peel back the layers of the superficial differences among them, they far more often than not reveal that same genuine, straightforward, empathetic, and warm-hearted spirit, the likes of which truly embody the storybook typecasts of "good people."

As my mother would wisely advise me someday, before I was to graduate college, a lot more of the world would open itself up to me because I had middle-American roots. People essentially like and trust people from the Midwest, and I must admit, my cornhusker heritage has served me well in this regard. There's no need to get into the minutiae of the past couple of decades, but time has proven her correct. Even so, that advice and three dollars would have bought me a pack of Camel Lights back then. If you were to give me Doc Brown's time machine and an irrefutable amount of hardcopy evidence of future happenings, there's no alternate universe where I could go back and convince young me of this– not on my dear mother's life.

Omaha was boring. It was cookie-cutter. We had no professional sports teams, and our only amusement park, Peony Park, was totally bitchin' if you happened to be a connoisseur of parks primarily consisting of rides that test the limits of G-Forces on the human body. NASA's best work couldn't outmatch the nauseating power of those puke-encrusted attractions, built and presumably last maintained in the early '60s. I'm still waiting for some Netflix exposé to blow the lid on the grossness.

And the weather distinctly sucked. There were like three or four pleasant weeks a year. The summers often hung out in the high 80s to low 90s range, but the permanent multiplier of 100% humidity rendered the region virtually uninhabitable for a whole season. (I know I'm weird, but I've never been a fan of mosquitos and my balls sticking to my leg.)

Before we went ahead and turned the thermostat up on the planet, the winters were frigid to the point of being polar. I recall numerous instances of getting school called off for days at a time when the wind chills would hit 40 to 50 below zero. Getting free days off of school notwithstanding, it was no fun, and neither was my limited conception of growing up where I did. Like my cousins, I wanted to grow up in Orange County, California. It was beautiful all year, and the entertainment value to a child was seemingly infinite.

Being the increasingly frustrated young teen I was circa 1997, I wasn't sure exactly how to express my brand of contrarianism at the time. I was a freshman at Burke High School, and for better or for worse, I happened to roll with the "cool kids" for the first two or three years. Although a large segment of them were legitimate athletes— as the '90s stereotypes would necessitate— I markedly was not. As previously explored, I had no desire whatsoever to play freshman football with my friends, but love the sport of football, I always have. Growing up in Nebraska during the Golden Years of Husker football pretty much dictated it as your birthright. And I was all for Big Red for the first 15 years.

I distinctly recall watching the 1994 National Championship win over Miami at my grandparents' communal watch party in their apartment complex and yelling my vocal cords silent. With even more clarity, I delightfully remember the 1995 clinic that the Blackshirts put on Danny Wuerffel's Florida Gators, which still stands as one of the largest displays of the chasm between #1 and #2 college football has ever seen. I loved those teams and that era of Husker football, indeed!— I sometimes fantasize about what I would and wouldn't do to have us magically catch that lightning ever again.

The problem was that I also arbitrarily picked up a taste for Michigan football at some point in third grade or so. It started as innocuously as me liking the team with the cool helmets. Then, after a few years of studying the Wolverines' rich history, both academic and football-related, I quickly adopted them as my primary rooting interest. By fifth grade, I could tell you everything about the program's history, each player on the two-deep, and the major stat lines of every game of the season. I became a total nerd for all things Michigan Wolverines.

And then the 1997 season happened. I'm willing to bet most of the people reading this won't have any idea to what I'm referring, so for you, here's your quick recap:

Michigan and Nebraska both finished the 1997 regular season of college football with undefeated records. Because of the structure of the bowl system of the time, Brian Griese, the QB of Michigan (not exactly a carbon copy of his NFL Hall-of-Fame dad), and his Wolverines were forced to play Ryan Leaf, the Washington State University QB (Google this dude's legacy), and his Cougars in the Rose Bowl. Scott Frost, Nebraska's native son and one-time mythical Husker QB (all of his coaching legacy conveniently omitted for brevity), and his Cornhuskers took on Peyton Manning, Tennessee QB and 1997 Heisman runner-up (not to mention 2021 NFL Hall of Fame Inductee), and his Volunteers in the Orange Bowl. In summary, Michigan barely slipped by WSU 21-16, and Nebraska utterly dismantled UT 42-17. Yes, I understand Michigan's Charles Woodson took the Heisman that season, and he will forever remain college football's all-around G.O.A.T. as it pertains to all three phases of the game. Even so, everyone knows that all other things being equal—

which they were– big-time football comes down to quarterback play, and Nebraska embarrassed a QB legend in their bowl game. Michigan barely outpaced a meme. You do the math. At the time, I refused to do any such thing.

Instead of applying the basic "eye test" to the situation, I subconsciously saw it as my chance to take up arms against all of the "sheeple" –as I most likely would've once viewed anyone of the local status quo– and lobby on behalf of Michigan being the true 1997-1998 Kings of College Football. And lobby, I did. I was loud, proud, and looking for anyone who wanted to hash things out verbally. I didn't know it then, but when I later went on to get a formal philosophy education, I learned that my efforts as a disgruntled football fan were born of a tactic called "sophistry." It's nothing more than the art of prosaically bullshitting your opposition to the point of tears. I went so far with my pursuit of becoming some bizarre iteration of a jock-wannabe and snowflake that I wrote a savage op-ed that I submitted to the *Omaha Jewish Press.* Fortunately, my steel trap of a memory naturally blocked out this public humiliation, but my mom still reminds me that it once transpired in time and space. [Hands over face]

All fandom aside, when the time came for me to apply for schools, you bet your ass UM was the alpha #1 application I sent out. The University of Florida, where my sister was a legacy and who ultimately accepted me, was a distant second. Colorado State University, some stoner state school out west, was just a convenient excuse for me to get out of senior English class one day in high school and listen to their sales pitch.

Regarding CSU, I essentially watched a 10-minute live-action infomercial, followed it up the next day with an in-person interview at a nearby seedy motel, and was accepted on the spot when I showed them a photocopy of my good (not excellent) transcript and copy of my even less impressive SAT scores. Getting a Blockbuster card was more difficult than getting into my alma mater.

When it all panned out, UM effectively told me to piss off. Florida was an unbearably humid proposition. And that CSU joint that accepts students like the armed forces, well, I heard they had some pretty good weed– way better than the seeded schwag we were used to in 1990s Omaha. I can't imagine the other dimension of existence where I was granted my first choice in the matter. It was the first traceable moment in my life of the cosmos knowing damn well what was better for my future than I did. Had Michigan accepted, I irrefutably would have obliged and lived in a positively different universe than the one where I now find myself. As it stands, I'm good with this particular plane of existence, warts and all.

In the years that have since passed, I hysterically laugh at my juvenile antics. On a global scale, I had zero-point-zero worldly problems. I was a cool kid but not the coolest. I was good with the ladies but not the best. I was relatively intelligent but finished 58th in a class of roughly 250-300, as I recall. Like so many people often tend to do, I didn't know how to be okay with just being okay at so many things. Instead of dedicating myself to discovering and fostering my true talents, I just found it easier to be generally disgruntled and take up contrarian points of view just for the sake of kicking up shit.

I'm no psychologist or sociologist or the like. Still, I'm reasonably sure the silly acrimony I created around two sports entities– both of which didn't and still don't even know I exist– was my closest teenage analog of a "goth phase." Instead of wearing black eye makeup and Marilyn Manson tee shirts, I took to the preppy's podium and spouted off a bunch of drivel just to get noticed, I've now come to realize. At least there are no damning pictures following me around of wonky haircuts messily draped over concertedly frowning faces– just some superfluous article yellowing in the archives of the *Omaha Jewish Press*.

I wouldn't call it the worst, but it definitely was one of the most superfluous of my life's various causes for which I've gone to battle.

And as we all age and hopefully learn from our precocious pasts, specific facts of matter become scathingly obvious. So before I step down from the preppy's podium of arbitrary, hypothetical, sporting rhetoric, I would like to go ahead and put it on public record that despite the current state of affairs, the 1997 Cornhuskers would have brained Michigan with the business end of the Sears Trophy. Also, I offer all apologies to the legendary Tom Osborne and Husker Nation. I now know what it is to be reborn. Thank you for your grace. [mic drop]

Skeleton

I have been told that everyone has "skeletons in the closet." Well, here's the gruesomest skeleton in mine.

Growing up, I was a pretty good kid. Notice I used the term "good" and not "nice". I mostly followed the rules. I respected my parents and the vast majority of my elders. I was studious. I was responsible and honest– as honest as any other kid– occasionally bending the truth to avoid punitive trouble. I didn't steal or wantonly destroy things. I didn't assault people or go out of my way to make anyone's life any more miserable than life can naturally be. By most comprehensive assessments, I was a good kid.

But I wasn't particularly nice. I blessedly was, and still very much am, surrounded by scores of people I consider my friends. With these individuals, maintaining the happy and positive nature of these relationships has never been overly strenuous. With them, it wasn't hard to be "good" or "nice." Sure, over the years, I've had my moments with each and everyone where my carnal desire to regress into "asshole mode"– born of fear or weariness– has overtaken my best attributes and intentions. Nonetheless, my inherent "goodness" or "decency" has traditionally trumped any such darkness or insensitive behavior.

I'm profoundly ashamed to profess to all that during my sophomore year of high school, I not only failed to be nice to someone who so desperately needed anything of the sort in his life but that I was an outright *ASSHOLE* to him. At age 41, I no longer wallow in such permanent shame and self-reproach that I can't openly share this story with the world. Nonetheless, it's taken me about 25 years to feel the self-awareness, impetus, accountability, and moral obligation to put it in print, regardless of how remorseful I've been for the past two and a half decades. This tragic tale must be told, however ugly and contemptible it may be. For what I cannot pay back to those I wronged,

I will forever try to pay forward to those of the same wretched circumstance of one of life's more unlivable dispositions.

For you to understand the nature of my transgression, it would be paramount to set the societal narrative of where I found myself when I was to perpetrate my willful shortcomings. It may all be painfully common knowledge, but its import bears worth discussing the social dynamics of what it meant to grow up a teen in the 1990s. Well before words like "inclusivity" became popularized mantras for American youth, teenagers were ruthlessly quick to categorize and stigmatize each other with cliche titles like: "geek," "stud," "jock," "queer," "hottie," "fatty," "dork," "skater," "fag," "freak," "druggy," "prude," "dude," "slut," "loser," or any other reductionist label best suited for one's most immediate judgmental needs.

Me? I could have assumed a few different labels. Still, by some stroke of fateful magic– I'm guessing my lifelong penchant for humor– when the junior high and high school years rolled around, I could brandish labels like "cool" or "partier." I was never a jock or physical specimen. I was never the pulse of the party scene, nor was I ever the one to have enough social clout to stir the pot and transform something previously pedestrian into something suddenly trendy. I was no social nexus at all. Still, I had all the necessary social stock to have friends on the football team, get invited to all the parties complete with booze and pot, and sit with all the popular kids at the lunch table or in the stands at inter-school competitions. For bringing little to the table other than my ability to hook up with pretty girls occasionally and often land wise-ass jokes– frequently at other peoples' expenses– I hit no minor jackpot in establishing an elevated foothold in the social hierarchy of a most stereotypical 1990's midwestern schooling experience.

But let's call a spade a spade. I was as insecure and in search of a rock-solid identity as the most awkward and socially inept of any of my classmates. I was a late bloomer, just discovering my long-awaited pubes somewhere midway through eighth grade, a sobering reality for someone as generally cocky and motivated by the affections of the opposite sex as any other of my peers. As previously noted, unlike virtually all of my athletic friends, I had a dad bod, and my metabolism wasn't improving with age. I might have had a little more experience with the ladies under my belt than the next guy, but for the next year, I would still be a virgin– the most indicting of all classifications for any straight, cis-gendered male of that era.

I successfully met most requirements for good standing in the teenage social sphere. Yet, I knew that I didn't have enough intangibles to preserve my social status without routine maintenance. What is "routine maintenance" exactly? I would argue that it is nothing more than maintaining the curated image that the "cool/popular" crowd wasn't as much a product of contrived illusions as it was a divine ordination and reflection of inherently "cooler"– thereby more "worthy"– socialites. It wasn't the trans-generational practice of peacocking by self-deluded teens. It was proliferating the mirage of the natural birthright of the social elite. It was a daily chore, and the parameters of its rule governed 24 hours a day and 365 days a year.

So it was under this prevailing social order and with this toxic mindset that I managed far too many of my behavioral decisions in those formative years of the mid-'90s to the early 2000s. If you were "cool," "popular," "happening," or your parents just happened to be out of town on the upcoming weekend, you were afforded membership into my universe. If you didn't, well, "Best of luck, but kindly go fuck yourself" was my subconscious social policy. If you weren't a blast to hang out with, you didn't maintain or bump my social stock by proxy, didn't provide the infrastructure for me and my "cool" friends to drink and get high, or you weren't the prospect of an attractive female for some sexual conquest, then you were seen as a detriment to my endeavors of such.

Not only was I not taking applications for new, random so-and-sos to be my friend, but I shamefully allowed lifelong friendships from as early as preschool to go unnurtured for years. That any of those guys are still of my beloved few "lifers" of friends– and some are– is one of the greatest reprieves I have ever received. But yes, the social aristocracy of my grade at Burke High School was firmly established, and anyone less than an enchanting transfer from another high school did not need to apply. All positions were adequately filled.

So it shouldn't come as any surprise that when I found myself in my Honors Chemistry class my sophomore year, I wasn't lobbying for inclusivity, equality, basic decency, or anything of the like. It was another class of my sixteen-year-old day and another on my high school transcript that seemed to have little bearing on the rest of my life. I could not have been more wrong.

Naturally, being one of the physical sciences, that class lent itself to a lab group format almost 50% of the time. The classroom had about 20 classic school desks arranged in the middle of the room, surrounded by eight lab tables for group exercises on the room's perimeter. The desks served as our permanently assigned seats, but whenever we went from lecture to lab, we were permitted to assemble ourselves at the tables in three to four-person lab groups. Mind you, none of my regular, weekend-worthy friends happened to be in my fourth-period chemistry class, but I did have a longtime respectful relationship with two of my classmates of many years, Mark and Kevin.

They didn't party or hold any sway with the ladies– the two most crucial requisites for vaunted social status– but they were pretty funny guys, and no one ever marked them as being of negative social value. As far as I was concerned, the three of us made for a formidable lab group whenever we needed to convene. Academically speaking, we all had roughly the same aptitude and scholastic performance, and socially speaking, they presented me with the workable possibility of a neutral popularity rating. It may have been ruthlessly crass, but that's just the way it was. That's the way *I was.*

But to our group's chagrin, Tyler wanted in. Tyler was a downright bizarre individual. If memory serves me correctly, he was relatively new to Burke, seeing as no one knew anything about him at the beginning of that tenth-grade year. He looked like a weirdo. He volunteered random anecdotes on non-sequitur topics. He constantly made cringeworthy jokes. He dressed like a tool. He didn't stand out as being overly bright—certainly not one you'd think would be in an honors class. He obviously had minimal self-esteem. He always seemed to be looking for external approval. He most likely had no friends. I couldn't imagine how he could; he had a prodigious superpower for making people uncomfortable enough to crawl out of their skin. He was the social "square peg" in a school full of "round holes." I might have been the roundest and biggest of those "holes."

It must have been early on in the semester when the exclusion began. I can't precisely recall the composition of the various lab groups in the room. Still, I can confidently say that the one that Mark, Kevin, and I had established was seemingly the most attractive to Tyler from an overarching perspective. From the outside looking in, we appeared as three approachable, happy guys. We were outwardly likable. We were fun and often brought back in line by our teacher, Mr. Pintursky, for enjoying ourselves too much and losing our primary focus. But we were as sharp as any other bunch in class, so our group grades were as boastful as the rest. Plus, there were only three of us, whereas most of the regular assemblies were maxed out at four. And without any reservations whatsoever, Tyler regularly attempted to join our group.

We collectively thwarted the first few attempts as cordially as we could. The three of us concocted increasingly spurious reasons why Tyler couldn't join our group. We started with excuses like the three of us were absolutely best friends, and we simply couldn't let anyone else into our circle of perfect exclusivity. Per our fabricated backstory, we had been besties since Kindergarten. After over a decade of operating as a seamless triumvirate, any rocking of our boat would most certainly end in unmitigated disaster.

At first, Tyler, as passive and insecure as he was, would sheepishly accept our blatant lies, thank us anyway, and slink off to sidle up to another group. The other groups weren't exactly clamoring for his membership, but none were ever so petty as to close their doors to him blatantly, shuttering him out into the cold abyss of peer-to-peer exile. Well, we did. And I was our ringleader.

Tyler either couldn't or wouldn't take a hint, and by the end of the first semester, our– or, more specifically, *my*– efforts to paint our lab group as patently unwelcoming had devolved from cordially civil to outright inflammatory. Rather than suggest we'd rather not upset our long-established apple cart, I had no problem eventually telling him like it was. He was weird. He made us uncomfortable. He made everyone uncomfortable. He was badgering in his insistence on being accepted, and this regular annoyance was essentially an opinion of the entire fourth-period class. Unlike everyone else in the class, including Mark and Kevin, I had the cold-blooded gall to enumerate those facts out loud and to his unwilling-to-accept face. On his very last attempt merely not to be the weirdo-loner he inevitably must have felt himself to be, I forever crushed his campaign by labeling him a "weasel," a constant pain in everyone's ass and one who could not figure out his social standing to save his life. In so many words, I explicitly implored him to fuck off and find a room full of other unlucky people to routinely inconvenience.

It was springtime later that year when I was sitting in Miss Wahler's second-period Spanish class, and the precursor beep that signals a school-wide announcement over the intercom signaled at a most improbable time of the morning. School announcements were almost exclusively made during homeroom hours or first period at the latest. That there was a beep around 9:30 was a most unorthodox occurrence, to be sure.

"Attention students: It is with great sadness and heavy hearts that we are informing you we received the notification this morning from the parents of sophomore Tyler Rasmussen that he has passed on and will no longer.............................."

As soon as I heard Tyler's name, all blood instantaneously drained from my four limbs, and my vision tunneled to a pinpoint focus down a tube of infinite nothingness. Everything beyond the utterance of the sterilized term "passed" fizzled into a haze of pure garble. I have no idea how the announcement finished, only that I was physically sick at the suspicion that this was no simple passing from a seizure or car accident or anything else of star-crossed happenstance. What began as a sickly fog quickly morphed into a silent but extraordinary panic. I hastily shoved my Spanish book and notes into my bag and told Miss Wahler I immediately had to go to the office in light of the vice principal's previous announcement.

Miss Wahler, likable and wholesome as she was, had never been confused with an intelligent woman. She often had lipstick on her teeth and a fractional understanding of the Spanish language compared to any other teacher in the department. Nonetheless, when she saw the look on my face, she must have intuitively known the magnitude of my demand. Not one to be pushed around by the assertive wills of her teenage subjugates, she didn't even blink at my proclamation. With a reflex of true compassion, she replied with a simple, "Of course."

When I finally got to the counselor's office, I was borderline hyperventilating as much from my hustle there as from the anticipation of the answers I was so desperately seeking in that manic moment. Seeing my obvious fluster of panic, the office secretary implored me to slow down and catch my breath– an existentially impossible proposition under the circumstances.

"I need to speak to Mr. Duggan right now," I insisted. "It's about Tyler Rasmussen."

Much like Miss Wahler, she didn't flinch in getting up and fetching my guidance counselor for me. Thankfully, he was readily available and invited me into his office promptly.

"How did Tyler die?" I bluntly commanded the question. "Did he kill himself?"

"Well, technically, I'm not at liberty to..." he started to reply when I authoritatively shut down his canned professional response in trying to maintain strict confidentiality.

Tell me! I shouted. I was never one to speak to my elders in such manners, much less my educators. But I didn't give two fucks if Mr. Duggan wanted to expel me and have me sent back to Kindergarten to repeat everything over again. I wasn't accepting his diplomatic approach. "I need to know." My desperation won over his diplomacy.

"Yes," the room echoed. "Tyler's parents informed us that he took his own life last night."

There are no words for the feeling of paralyzing guilt that washed over every last cell of my teenage life force at that very moment. It was a good thing I was already sitting, as I can only imagine I might have collapsed into a pile of molten shame right there on my guidance counselor's office floor. For an administrator I until moments before found to be of virtually no use to me, he immediately became an indispensable incinerator into which I would cast the despicable narrative I not only fostered but, to a large degree, orchestrated in our fourth-period chemistry class.

It is of a profoundly dark rendition of serendipity that the least honorable thing I was ever to do in my life had transpired in an "honors" class. Whatever honor and class I may have felt myself ever to have were suddenly vanquished and relegated to the halls of eternal disgrace. Every one of Mr. Duggan's assurances felt like a God damn lie. I suppose I wasn't a murderer or child abductor or anyone else of calculated evil. Nonetheless, one of my peers was dead by his own hand, and I, in no conceivable way, had made his decision any more difficult. If anything, I was another contributing factor to making it that much easier.

Given the situation, Mr. Duggan let me spend the rest of the second and third periods in the counselor's office to regain some semblance of composure. Unavoidably, I was eventually forced back into the scheduled flow of my school day, off to fourth-period Honors Chem.

Immediately upon crossing the threshold into the classroom, a palpable force of regret permeated the air. We all shuffled into class in our typically staggered order, each quieter and more somber than the next. Even Mr. Pintursky, the quintessential old, crotchety, no-nonsense grouch, was slow to his game plan. Never having had anything remotely resembling "bedside manner," he authentically did his best to address the dinosaur-sized vacuum in the room– the vacant space where Tyler used to sit.

After his surprisingly eloquent recognition of our communal loss, he continued with the week's lesson plan in whatever unit we were studying. The rest of the class, presumably grieving Tyler in their respective ways, pulled out their comp books and continued with Pintursky– not Mark, Kevin, or myself. No. We sat at our lab table in silence, each of us lamenting ourselves and the roles we played in those very seats. For almost 50 minutes, the three of us would not pick up a pen, open a book, or mind a word about the chemical breakdown of the natural world around us. Conscribed to our triad of remorse, all rules of chemical composition and preservation of matter were of zero value. We felt like monsters, and I was the alpha.

For the better part of an entire school year, I played my part, and an active one at that, to keep an awkward kid of cringe-worthy proportions at a distance so that I wouldn't lose "social equity" by associating with him in chemistry class. I'm not going to completely vilify my juvenile self by purporting to have been a supreme perpetrator of patent "bully" status. I never went out of my way to make his life hell. I had no scores to settle or anything of the like. I didn't actively choose him as a target for comedic ridicule. I simply didn't want him in my sphere of existence, and when he failed to read the room and see his place in the social pecking order, I employed the monster within to run him off with pitchforks. Rather than abide by the "Golden Rule" and merely allow this troubled spirit to be himself– obtrusively awkward and all– I chose the opposite. I let my insecurities, imperfections, and fear of isolation weaponize my faculties of alienation. Instead of giving him refuge from his unlivable world of torment, I erected a fortress around my shortcomings and shooed him back out into the wilderness alone.

In the time that has passed, I have learned to forgive myself to some degree. I know we are all responsible for our own decisions, and he chose to end his life. I didn't make that choice for him. In the same light, I will forever hold myself accountable for the decisions I did and didn't make regarding Tyler. Yes, I was still technically a kid myself. It didn't matter. I was old enough to know better. I knew damn well that not only do sticks and stones break bones, but that particularly incisive words can destroy someone. I wasn't self-aware enough to realize it at the time, but the arrested development of my teenage sense of empathy caused me to react in the nasty, fearful way I did. I was in no way a finished product in any regard when it came to emotional maturity. I had my own neuroses and curated facade to deal with. I was effectively drowning in an ocean of teenage angst, and I had no problem holding someone else's head under the surface to prop myself up another smidge above the waterline.

Additionally, it was posthumously brought to my attention that he was apparently having significant issues at home, waffling between the respective custodies of his divorced parents. His home life was rumored to be even more dogshit than his school life. In a small measure, that made me feel a tad less culpable. In a more considerable measure, it made me that much more regretful that his life was so ostensibly godawful to begin with. Everything about it was a tragedy.

And this is why I write this essay. What I can't repay Tyler or his family, I hope to pay forward to the world with this story. It will forever remain a "black eye" when I look into the mirror of my soul. Black eyes aren't fatal, and they don't tell a whole story. But black eyes, when seen as reminders of our darkest deeds, can also remind us that our fight to be bigger than our inner monsters can be won. Much like actual warfare– as it is a war for one's moral legacy– it's a series of battles, some won and some lost. Unfortunately, it's not as linear of a trajectory as we would hope it to be. I wish I could say that after that day of Tyler's death, I was inscrutably friendly and overtly inclusive of everyone who would cross my path. I've lost some battles to the monster within in the time since. Even so, the indelible black eye of my treatment of Tyler has helped fuel my life's conquest to, in some way, right my wrongs.

For some time now, it has not been acceptable just to be a "good" guy deep down. Sure, being a generally solid human, dutiful friend, good samaritan, respectful child, etc., is essential for cultivating one's humanity. But those attributes are not sufficient unto themselves. Being generally "good" isn't the most confounding of ambitions for those with adequate mental faculties and who are born into semi-decent families. A little bit of the right nature combined with just enough of the proper nurture seems to generate typically well-intended, though terminally short-sighted and self-centered human beings. I would argue these individuals sufficiently check in as "good," however ungracefully they may or may not go about their days. Humans are humans, and some of us, frankly, are much more myopic than others. Learning to view people of this ilk more as imperfect creatures than wilfully-strategic, ingenious assholes seems to be the most logical approach. It's a much more palatable viewpoint than holding your average human to idealistic standards and then getting bent out of shape when they invariably disappoint.

But being "nice" is a whole different ballgame. Nice requires patience. It requires selflessness. It requires the subject first to be nice to oneself before ever being reflexively kind to others. And the truth is that I've not typically been overly kind to me. I've always been my own biggest critic. Far overshooting the virtue of humility, ever since I was a child, I have struggled, like so many others, with having to learn to love the man in the mirror. And for years and years, I just didn't. I pretended I did. I went through the motions as though I did. I might have even convinced myself that I did. But I didn't.

And so now, as I see it, my redemption arc has begun with the pursuit of "nice." As previously noted, it hasn't been a perfect incline on the algebraic X-Y coordinate graph. For every couple of moments of active kindness I've consciously exercised, I've had a setback, reverting to the reactive animalistic nature within. But I am happy to say that each time I catch myself in the act of losing my battle to the monster, it gets that much easier to reel it back in and break its will for future uprisings. And in this oscillating journey of self against self, I find my reprieve.

In Tyler's name and with his cataclysmic legacy, I push forward each day, challenging myself to find unique ways to bring light and positivity to those in my orbit. This lifelong commitment has even materialized itself in me as currently building a career as an End-of-Life doula, giving comfort and dignity to those in the twilight of their lives. At 16, no one in this solar system would have ever confused me with someone who would someday get his kicks by hanging out with hospice patients on their deathbeds. But I do. I don't know that there is any correlation or causation between my treatment of Tyler and my recent reconfiguration of my life's purpose, but I'd like to think there might be.

Nonetheless, my reparations are underway. My odyssey from Asshole to Zachary has evolved from a hapless fandango to an all-consuming evolution of spirit. If I die cold, alone, broke, and naked by making this my lifelong endgame, then I'm okay with that. God knows that is a quantum distance from the oblivion of boundless regret. Tyler Rasmussen, wherever you are on the other side of the veil of perception, I hope you are finally at peace. Our legacies are forever intertwined. May your memory eternally drive me to be better than I once was. With infinite regret for the experience and endless appreciation for the lesson, I hope to make good on your story and have it eternally serve as a reminder that life is a series of choices. Those choices ultimately determine the legacy we leave behind. Are we the "good" and "nice," or are we the embodiment of the "monster" within?

The unfolding narrative marches on in perpetuity.

Third World Royalty: Part 1

It's not often one can locate in their memory two of the most inspiring passing strangers they had ever met in their own developmental histories.

Well, I can. It was the first week of July 2005 when I set off on my post-college graduation backpacking trip. It was me and my trusty backpack, shoestringing around the bulk of Western Europe for two months or so. I recall hitting 10 or 11 countries thanks to the Eurail pass– the golden ticket to riding Europe's expansive railroad network. I couldn't tell you precisely what my endgame was. However, at the time of my graduation from Colorado State University, I was still very high on the teachings of my philosophy and creative writing education. Having adopted this romanticized notion of riding the rails of Europe– reminiscent of my Beat Writer hero, Jack Kerouac– I longed to travel by whim, extemporaneously exploring the universe at hand. That, paired with my inherent reverence for ancient Greek philosophy, would have me conjure up some half-baked fantasy of making my way to the lands of Socrates and Plato and having some sort of contrived revelation as to what I should do with my life. But first things first. A guy had to celebrate a little, putzing around on the way to ultimate enlightenment.

So, after landing in London and a solid night of painting the town with fellow youth hostel roommates, I made my way to Harwich, England, to catch my ferry to the promised land– Amsterdam. Why a "promised land," you may ask? Well, for a cannabis-crazed youth, perplexed by the classical American prohibition of the plant, this Amsterdam place was a mythical place for me at that juncture in human history. It would still be another four years or so until I would procure my first medical marijuana red card in San Diego and eight until I would work as a commercial grower in Denver. So, for there to be a land where one could publicly consume cannabis and not incessantly have to look over one's shoulder for law enforcement was simply a fantastical notion of a place that couldn't possibly exist. Yet, exist it did, and I found it.

As it would turn out, for this counter-clockwise journey around the bulk of Europe, I would visit Amsterdam both at the beginning and the end of my European trip. I explored almost every coffee shop in the northern third of the city, including ground zero– the Red Light District. If it was green and got me lit, then by God, I wanted to consume it. Of course, that area is also notoriously iconic for hard drugs, sex shows, prostitution, and debauchery of all imaginable sorts. Honestly, I couldn't have cared any less for that scene. Sure, walking to see the scantily clad ladies pervading the storefront windows had its inherent and ostentatious draw to the philandering twenty-two-year-old me. Hell, some of them were beyond gorgeous and mildly tempting.

Nevertheless, I could never in my life bring myself to the point of having to make a monetary transaction for skin-on-skin relations. I can't say I blame any person who wants to partake in boosting their local sex economy, but fortunately, I've never had to resort to such measures. Even so, chivalry wasn't my younger self's strong suit, and I couldn't help but scope out the market. It was an alien moonscape compared to Old Town Fort Collins and a scene that required my bearing witness. But Amsterdam was an enigma that wasn't exactly forwarding the narrative of me achieving an intrinsically valuable purpose for my quest. I knew I had to get along with my travels.

As I extracted myself from that complete and utter distraction of a metropolis, I made haste down south. Having already been to France as a teen, I wasn't overly intent on spending much time there. As far as I was concerned, it was a lovely revisit but more of a space for passing through than a destination in and of itself. What it would afford me would be a gateway into Italy, a country semi-exotic to a hick

Nebraskan like myself, rife with the historical narrative of the modern world as we know it.

Essentially living up to the mythological hype of my imagination, the ruins of Ancient Rome, the canals of Venice, and even that architectural abomination of a structure in Pisa, that place had largely been what I had always imagined it to be. Well, except that, ironically enough, the single worst slice of pizza I've ever eaten in my four decades of existence on this planet was from a spot right there in the shadow of the Leaning Tower itself.

Of all of my travails in that country, the place which I found to be most novel was Cinque Terra, a series of five fishing villages, connected by hiking trail, boat, or train only, and quaintly set upon the coast of the Italian Riviera. Having glommed on to another group of American travelers for a few days, we progressively hiked our way from town to town, enjoying to no end the rustic micro excursion of this furtively nestled stretch of coastline. The food was nothing short of exquisite. Each village had its offerings of fresh pasta and even fresher seafood. The ristorantes were nothing more than cafes by American measures, which is to say, perfectly intimate, charming, and authentic in ways that I've since found hard to discover outside of Europe.

Naturally, a scene as described would inherently be occupied by noticeably warm and welcoming countryfolk. Chronologically, I had yet to make it to Rome at that point in my journey, so it didn't strike me exactly how much I would come to appreciate those rural Italians infinitely more than those I encountered in Rome. Sure, generalized statements will always have their exceptions. That said, I recall loving the architecture and history of Rome while also primarily being unenamored with most of its citizens, or at least the characters I encountered along the way. I don't have any specific instances to note, just a general succession of occurrences leading me to believe that the average Roman I encountered was transparently more pissed off than your average NYC subway commuter. Indicting.

That was inconsequential as I saw it. Rome was for the birds, both its contemporary and ancient versions. Greece. Now, that's where a real existentialist would hang his hat, right? For the very place that would birth the concepts of objective moral virtue and mathematical calculations of verbal reason would inevitably hold the answer to my own personal $64,000 question: What the fuck was I supposed to do with the rest of my post-college life? Undoubtedly, the same land on which stood the remains of The Forum would also have to inspire me from cerebral dope smoker to professional philosopher, right? (Right??)

Ha!!

No such luck. Sure, I would tour the Parthenon. I would explore the entirety of the Acropolis. I would pay homage to the legendary Mt. Olympus. It was all empty to me. I couldn't tell you why I had this overriding and eternal pull to Greece for the latter half of my undergraduate education, but I did. I felt as though the missing piece of me was somewhere to be found in this historically dynamic geo-locale, as if it harbored some sort of ethereal and transformative energy I could find nowhere else. But it was just another sprawl of civilization with a few ancient buildings, a decaying infrastructure, rampant pollution, cantankerous city dwellers, and mazes of tourist traps. I heard their economy sucks too. But what do I know?

Hoping the Isles would offer some comforting reprieve from my existential disappointments, I traveled down to Paros with a hippie Canadian couple, Sam and Alex. It's irrelevant, but I always find it funny to point out regarding a couple with androgynous names that Sam was the girl, and Alex was the guy. I will admit that after spending most of the previous three weeks traveling alone, it was indeed a delight finding these two when I did. True to form, the painfully genuine and disarmingly friendly Canadian charm was a bit of an elixir. Traveling with them allowed me to relax and feel as though real people had my back as I was out in the world's diaspora. It may sound stupid, but being able to do something as simple as getting up from a cafe table to go the bathroom and not having to strap on your backpack (entire life) every single time was an invaluable novelty for this lonesome traveler.

We spent a few days exploring the island, lounging on the beach, and eating some of the best Mediterranean food I've ever had to this day. After about a week of this respite with my two new friends, I got the burn to get back to the mainland and hit the rails once again. Those two opted to stay back and were planning on looking for under-the-table work to keep themselves there indefinitely– something I initially wanted to do myself. But sitting still was never exactly my strong suit. And I did what I often tend to do and bounced. [I still wonder what happened to those hippies. I hope they went on to make several dreadlocked, patchouli-smelling children. Bless their swollen Canadian hearts.]

Port of Patras.

I had been in Greece for a week and a half, maybe two weeks at this point, and I knew I had to forage onward and away from this self-induced disappointment of a country. I'm not sure what I was looking for, but it definitely wasn't there in Greece– except that, fatefully, it happened to be departing this land on the same freighter as myself.

In fourth grade, my father took us on a Carnival Cruise in the Caribbean. The ship was named *The Ecstasy*, if I'm not mistaken. At the time, it was about as decadent of a vessel as a middle-class guy like my old man could afford to treat his family. It was complete with buffets, casinos, shopping, performance theaters, waterslides, and all the bells and whistles one could hope for in 1992. Well, this ship was distinctly not that.

It was an old-looking freighter of mixed-use, ostensibly having moved passengers and cargo back and forth across the Adriatic Sea for decades. She looked stout and reliable, and she was my quickest way to get back to Italy and the meat of the continent. Yet, based on my highly skewed, pre-conceived notion from childhood, this was not what I had envisioned for my international ocean travel. Furthermore, the posters in the ticketing office in Paros influenced my expectations, which certainly suggested something more in line with my pampered ten-year-old memories. A massive freighter she was, indeed. It looked as though the rust on the outer shell had been painted white a thousand times over, rendering a subtle zebralike pattern of burnt orange down her sides. Save for the blue of the Greek flag proudly jutting from the center mast, she bore no other colors whatsoever. She was spartan, much like the legends of her banner's ancient historical lore.

I recall embarking onto the ship via a drawbridge leading directly into the cargo hull. Optics weren't even an afterthought. The only analogy I can think of is like entering a restaurant through the back alley emergency exit, squeezed haphazardly between two overflowing dumpsters. Passengers were to shuffle between narrow rows of pallets layered 20-30 feet high. Cars were loaded on top of cars, and many were packed to the top of the windshield with personal storage. Porters hustled up and down the alternate pallet rows, pushing dollies stacked with wooden boxes twice their height– contents unknown. I can only imagine there was a more appropriate entrance for higher-paying passengers, though this was the route for plebian travelers like myself.

Eventually, a narrow, musty staircase would guide us to the vessel's top deck. Though there was a somewhat sizeable indoor area with basic seating, a few rickety tables, and a snack bar hocking price-gouged cheeseburgers of a quality on par with one's local penitentiary, the majority of the ship's few hundred passengers were ultimately forced to mill about the open-air deck. They oversold the voyage by at least double– that is, if creature comforts were to be considered. They weren't. But, for the most part, it was a delightful proposition, spending the better part of a 16-hour voyage in the European August evening, feeling the breeze of the Adriatic washing my disappointments away with the currents.

Once I got a feel for what I had to work with, I made my way to an outdoor patio table towards the stern of the ship. I plunked my 40-pound pack on the table, lit up an American Spirit cigarette, and pulled out my Rand McNally foldable map of Europe. Naturally, this was well before navigation was as easy as conjuring up Google Maps from the wizard paddle in one's pocket, and the best technology for me actively tracking my journey was a ballpoint pen set upon the slick paper of an old-school map. I had spent most of my waking hours the past few weeks with the Canadians, so I mainly neglected this downtime ritual. After a few minutes of intently examining the map, retracing every step of my journey to that point, I looked up across the patio and saw some guy who already had his eyes set on me. Most of the time, when one man looks up to lock eyes with another strange man across a room, things typically get weird or sideways rather quickly. For whatever reason, this mutual recognition was patently not that. Almost as soon as mutual acknowledgment was made, he cracked a massive smile, got up from his table, and walked toward me.

"You look like a guy who might be able to spare a cigarette," he suggested in an indistinguishable and highly viscous Eastern European accent. I didn't flinch. I pulled a smoke from my pack and rolled it across the table to where he was now seated. "Your shirt," he said, pointing to my tie-dye Grateful Dead t-shirt. "That's the shirt my kind of person wears. I saw you when you sat down and knew you were my kind of guy."

"Oh ya? What kind of guy is that?"

"A colorful traveler, like myself," he quipped.

"Colorful" isn't exactly the word I would have used to describe this individual. Appearing to be roughly a couple of years older than me (27 or 28, I think), he was a bit of an eclectic mess. His billowy pants barely fit his rail-thin frame, fastened precariously to his body with what appeared maybe to be a woman's belt. His shirt was tight, weathered, and covered with a cheap but new-looking hoodie. He was wielding a pink Minnie Mouse backpack with once-bright purple straps, now covered in a thin layer of oily grime. His hair was long, about halfway down his back, and he rocked a relatively thick yet scraggly beard. He appeared as though he hadn't showered in a week or two, though fortunately, he didn't stink. His general appearance would be best described as a contemporary version of a twenty-something Jesus Christ, spending his summer as a hodgepodge beach bum.

He pulled out a tattered book of matches with one red-headed soldier left and lit my offering. That he managed to effortlessly achieve this despite the whipping winds of the top deck was a mild miracle, a defiance of physics no seasoned smoker could ever imagine. I didn't know it yet, but it was simply a tiny harbinger of what I would later recognize as his otherworldly nature.

"Davorin," he proclaimed, extending his hand for the shaking. "Davorin Gazalan."

"Zach Perelman," I replied, extending my own to meet his titanesque grip. Although he looked like he weighed a buck thirty soaking wet, he had the hand strength of Andre the Giant. As it would turn out, Davorin was from the village of Dubrovnik in Slovenia. According to him, Slovenia, much like himself, was a nation of impoverished but wildly happy citizens. This jovial disposition would probably explain his penchant for audibly chuckling after every other statement. Though he insisted that he was a citizen of the proverbial third world– hailing from a family of peasant farmers– not for one moment did his energy or spirit match his description of the overwhelming despair from where he originated. How could it? As he described his home village conditions of abject poverty and political corruption, he punctuated nearly every statement with a defiant chuckle, as if to say "Fuck You" to the idea of adversity. He also just plain old loved to use the word "Fuck" a whole lot– but always accompanied with a wholesome, chuckling smile. Either he was batshit crazy or one of the single most well-adjusted humans I would ever meet.

After a few minutes of initially feeling each other out, he cut right to the chase. "You smoke hash or what, man? I got this ball of Moroccan black tar in Athens, and it's lasting way longer than I thought it would."

If Jerry Garcia himself had resurrected and offered the same proposition, I'm not sure I could have been more excited. At this juncture, I hadn't had a burn since stomping out my last joint in the Amsterdam train station roughly three weeks earlier, and every cell in my body was clamoring at the prospect of getting reacquainted with my old medicinal friend. An assertive yes was my reply, and with that, as though he had an intimate understanding of the ship, he led me into the indoor corridor, down a conspicuously hidden service staircase, and out a side door leading to a private deck. Out, he popped the goo ball, about the size of a grape. He unfurled his mostly empty bag of loose-leaf rolling tobacco and some Tops papers and rolled up a funny cigarette within 30 seconds or less. He didn't bat an eye at the prospect, but I've always been a bit of a coward when it comes to defiance of authorities, and God knows I couldn't imagine having to call my parents to spring me from a Greek or Italian prison for smoking doobies. It was a Greek ship, but we were on our way to Italy, and the Italians do *not* fuck around when it comes to prosecuting drug offenders, even petty cannabis users. In my previous foray through Italy, I was approached in various train stations on no fewer than three occasions by police with circling drug dogs as my long-haired, tie-dye, and backpack-wearing self traveled from city to city. Despite my typically paranoid pot smoker tendencies, Davorin's happy-go-lucky bravado forcibly put me at ease. We rendered his artwork to ash in maybe twice the time it took him to manufacture it. Poof, and into the sea, the roachy evidence was cast.

As previously mentioned, Davorin came from the humblest of means. Despite the fact that his parents could hardly keep food on the table or heat in their one-bedroom domicile for six (including his wife and young boy), Davorin never let his financial hardships keep him from traveling the rails. Armed with a Slovenian passport in his young teens, he would begin his rucksack life with impromptu weekend trips to Croatia and Austria. Those trips, in time, evolved into more extensive, multi-week excursions, ultimately having him visit every continental European country by age 19. I never got a straightaway answer as to how, even in a developing nation, parents would have such a free-range approach to parenting that he could get away with this. The best I could deduce was that perhaps there were places still on this wild planet where people were conditioned to the realities of this life "the old-fashioned way." By all means, it sounded as if he came from a notably healthy and supportive family unit– albeit one subsisting below our ordinary conception of the poverty level. Perhaps the daily scrapping for survival forged a collective strength that naturally imbued them with this sense of having absolutely nothing to lose. If your kids can laugh in the face of life's most brutish struggles, then surely they must be able to freeload their way around the world as openly as feral birds!

This was his logistical approach: freeloading. Now, most of us would naturally associate the term "freeloading" to be of a most disreputable nature. I would argue that this would most certainly be the case for those born of first-world means and opportunities. In this instance, Davorin was in no way a lazy or parasitic element of the sort. Despite his most precarious existence, he was genuinely kind, lovable, charming, seemingly fearless, and unrelentingly optimistic. His was the heart of famed world explorers, yet the socioeconomic factors at play would cage that drive if that heart were to belong to most other men. But Davorin had a heart unlike any other that I have ever met, even at the very moment of writing this.

At the time of recanting his life and current journey, Davorin had precisely eight Euros in his pocket. He started with 40 about two weeks earlier. With this being the case, he invested the minimum in a ticket to get out of the country, but once he made it out of Slovenia, he would never pay another rail fare again. For those who don't know how it works, riding the rails requires the rider to purchase a ticket in advance and freely embark upon the train when it arrives at the station. Anyone can walk on the train, but the onus is legally on the rider to ensure they made the proper transaction before boarding. Eventually, an usher walks from railcar to railcar, checking tickets to ensure all passengers follow protocol appropriately. Violators would inevitably be fined for considerably more than the cost of the original fare of the ticket and/ or jailed if one went rogue and became a repeat offender.

Davorin learned at a young age to be rogue but be so damn lovable in the process that all but one time, he managed to escape a fine. His strategy in riding the rails was relatively simple yet brilliant. He noted that Slovenian is not only an uncommon language for most Europeans to speak but that people from his particular region had a little something extra in their difficulty being understood outside of the area. He spoke not only his native tongue but also English and German with perfect ease. The authorities didn't need to know that. Being the minimalist he was, he usually only traveled with two sets of clothes, a toothbrush, toothpaste, and a bar of soap. Those items would occupy roughly a quarter of a standard-sized backpack. He would then stuff his pack to the brim with a litany of nonsense: crumbled maps, old rail tickets (expired ones he'd found in the trash, naturally, but imposed to suggest he was typically a do-gooder consumer), food wrappers, drawings made by his kid (selling his family-man appeal), an open and spilling plastic baggie with both pistachios and discarded shells spewing all over the place, etc.

Whenever an usher would approach him and ask for a ticket, Davorin had a perfectly practiced spiel of putting on a genuine smile while rummaging through the pockets of his person as though he was searching for his ticket. While this first phase would transpire over a minute or two, he would persist in speaking his unique dialect of Slovenian in an increasingly rapid and slightly more panicky tone, as though he legitimately lost the ticket he had *just* bought. Because most ushers were essentially softies and because none of them could understand him, the majority would often just pass him by once they saw how bent out of shape this parody of a "poor, ignorant Slovenian" must be.

He would resort to his bag of nonsense for those who weren't placated with this first display of confusion. Unzip it fast. Spread the junk as far and frantically around the railcar as possible. Rummage and panic– while *never* dropping his sympathizable, nervous smile– and wait for the usher's level of neuroses to out sweat his own. Rinse. Repeat. This cheeky ploy would see my friend thousands and thousands of miles around the continent over the years. And from what I understand, that one fine he did receive (between Slovakia and Poland years earlier) was laughed away, much like most of this man's earthly problems seemed to be.

Well, this particular European foray of his had some fun curveballs up to the point of our meeting on the freighter. As he recanted, it was only two days and a couple hundred miles into the trip when he hit his first snag. His trusty bag of shenanigans (and a few necessities) was lifted off his sleeping lap while riding the overnighter from Prague to Munich. Despite my knowledge of the contents of that bag, I couldn't help but personally shudder at the thought of losing my own bag in all of this. It was my lifeline to everything– save for the passport and few hundred Euros' worth of traveler's checks in my waistband wallet. Not only did he seem not to lament his recanted misfortunes, but he laughed it off harder than any other statement I had heard him make in knowing him the past hour or so. It was a full-on belly laugh in the face of what most lonesome travelers like myself would consider detrimental to the endgame.

"Fucking thieves, man," he quipped. "I hope they enjoy my shitty underwear and pistachio shells. And now, I get to wear this stupid fucking thing," he giggled as he gestured towards his backpack, the stuff of an 8-year-old girl's dreams. "Ya, when I got to my hostel that night, I told my story to a bunch sitting around the lobby bar. Before I knew it, the bartender went to the back storage area and emerged with this bag plus a tee-shirt from lost and found. He also 'forgot' to charge me for my beers. These three Japanese guys gave me underwear, socks, and body wash. A local German gave me this sweatshirt off of his back. Some Spaniard gave me her toothbrush. I don't give a shit that it was used. She was hot. Her boyfriend gave me his toothpaste. Some large British man donated the pants, and his wife donated the belt. A Turkish lady about 60 years old and who lived around the corner practically tried to adopt me. She ended up giving me a free room and cooked me three meals daily for a week and a half. I couldn't tell if she wanted me as a son or as a lover, but she didn't want me to go when I did." With this proclamation, he fiercely laughed well beyond a chuckle once again.

It was becoming evident to me at this point. As a devout believer in soft determinism– a fate we can somewhat control–I believe I was drawn to Greece in the first place, simply to leave it and find this irreplicable character in the process. It was rare in that time of my life to sit and listen– not just awaiting my chance to speak– but to sponge every last neutron of meaning from the individual opposite me. Yet, his presence rendered me a captive audience. All I had were questions and charitable offerings. Much like the aforementioned players in his happy-go-lucky drama, I couldn't help but have this burning desire to give him what I had to share. I bought us a couple of shitty burgers and bags of potato chips from the snack bar twice before our sea voyage ended. Add to that a couple of beers. I would unsolicitedly hand him cigarettes as regularly as I'd smoke them myself, allowing him to conserve his own looseleaf tobacco for leaner times. I insisted he call and check in with his wife on my international cell phone– a dollar-per-minute undertaking in 2005. On principle, I split my food stash of a loaf of bread, Nutella, dried fruit, and salted almonds with him. Frankly, I was traveling on my Westernized concept of a shoestring budget. However, something about Davorin's infectious spirit coaxed me into a state of inspired giving myself, born out of this contagion of fearlessness.

His bravado and intrepid will to unconditional positivity were nothing short of intoxicating. Never had giving away my personal possessions felt so much like the honor and privilege described by conventional ethics as when I was giving this and that to Davorin. Contributing to his fanciful dance around Europe hardly felt like charity. Moreover, it felt like a contribution to the hero's journey, to the triumph of Faith over Fear. Davorin was no charlatan. He lived squarely in the moment and embraced the idea that so long as he had a breath in his body and a person to relate to, his trajectory would be forever safe within the safety net of universal human connection.

Before we knew it, the freighter had docked in Brindisi, Italy. The overnight was a bit of a savage sleep. Of course, Davorin and I had stayed up far later than most, jabbering away and chain-smoking. So, by the time we went to lay out sleeping bags– or, in his case, a tarp we found in a janitor's closet amongst some cleaning supplies– the entirety of the enclosed indoor area of the ship was covered with sleeping bodies. We could hardly get to the bathrooms, much less sweep out a few square feet to lay down and join the rest. We proceeded to find a windy corner of the partially enclosed deck outside of the snack bar and froze our asses off until sunrise. Perhaps Mediterranean summers are toasty hot during the days, but the whipping winds of the Adriatic at night were no joke. We both awoke shivering, but we had made it. Mainland Europe. A cigarette and Nutella sandwich for breakfast, and we were off.

As we disembarked the ship, Davorin shot me a devious glance accompanied by his typical chuckle. Knowing how enchanted I was with his disposition to defy logic and peril with love and humor, he said softly, "Fucking watch this." True to their training, the Italian Port Authority had a few policemen herding drug-sniffing German Sheppards among the throngs of people as they hastily spewed from the hull of the ship. Knowing damn well that the ball of hash in his pocket would get the dogs hot and huffy, he proceeded to leisurely stroll with the bulk of the masses, within two feet of and in between two separate dogs, as though he knew his overall juju would somehow rouse their instincts without pinpointing the source of the contraband. Of course– it worked.

As the permanent worrier I am, as soon as I saw him needlessly tempting the fate of sleeping in an Italian prison, I hustled to the far side of the exodus of passengers. That way, I could wait and watch Davorin from a safe distance. I hurried, set up shop a hundred yards away, and looked back to watch the scene unfold. He leisurely split the dogs– chuckling as always– and slowly walked in my direction with both palms up to the sky as to say, "What were you worried about, you pussy?"

No less than five seconds after he passed, his downwind funk hit the dogs, setting them off in an alarmingly loud frenzy. Rather than shake down the hobo-looking Jesus impersonator with the pink and purple Minnie Mouse backpack who walked by just a moment earlier, the three cops turned on the adjacent family (or so they appeared to be) and stopped them in their tracks for what I can only imagine to be a prolonged search of them and their abundant luggage. Davorin didn't look back for a second. As soon as the dogs started barking, he could no longer hold his mischievous delight to himself and broke out into laughter, the volume of which was hardly masked by the fracas of barking K-9s behind him. Unflinchingly free was this man.

Having made our way further from the port and into the city of Brindisi, my paranoia of traveling with a hash smuggler– as Italian authorities would've indubitably considered him– began to wane significantly. Soon enough, we would burn through the rest of his stash as we cruised a few back alleys and awaited our early afternoon train out of town. I was happy to help lighten the load and even more delighted to have all evidence of wrongdoings up in smoke and out of our collective possession. He and I were traveling north on the rails and decided to stick together until we had to go our own separate ways. At least now, I was perfectly lit up for my trip to Bologna. Yet, I was no longer afraid of a potential fourth shakedown in an Italian train station.

In perfect accordance with relativity and the idea that time is fleeting when one is divinely enjoying one's company, the train ride was over like that. With half a pack of smokes between the two of us, a couple of Nutella sandwiches, and numerous tales of adventure, seven hours disappeared like that. Of course, he never bought a ticket, and karma would have the ushers somewhere else on that ride– no scenes of frazzled but friendly Slovenian journeymen for me to witness.

[It should be noted that Davorin made his Nutella sandwich using the raw, dirty train car seat next to him as his preparation platform. For someone who earlier indicated to me that he adamantly wouldn't bite his nails "because of all the shit underneath," he seemed to have no problem eating right off of that fart filter of a seat. Perhaps it was somewhat paradoxical, but for a bit of a germophobe like myself, it was renegade, I tell you.]

As the train pulled into the Bologna station, bittersweet was my realization that my time traveling with Davorin had rapidly ended. He was now just a couple of hours from home and looking to get back east to his wife and kid after surviving another improvised fandango around the continent. I was fixed on getting back to Switzerland. Having buzzed through it on my impetuous hustle to Greece, I wanted to revisit Interlaken and some adjacent Swiss Villages to spend a little time in the high country of the Alps. The time had come to disembark and go our separate ways.

It was a moment truly unlike any other in my life. I was a young man at a particularly murky point in life, graduating college– the life of academia, ideals, romanticism, virtue, legend, storied existences, and limitless potential. I was faced with the fear of the reality of leaving all of that behind to join "the real world." The real world was where one must show up daily to earn one's keep. It is a place of burden, pain, compromise, disappointment, and the like, and I had subconsciously feared making this transition for some time.

It wasn't until I met this character named Davorin Gazalan a mere 26 hours earlier that I was gifted with proof in the flesh that one can live in that place of idealism and simultaneously take on the perils of the world at large. He was a walking tapestry of human compassion, adorned with the donated clothes of those whose lives he touched in one way or another. Not only did he not begrudge having less money to his name than most people spend on a sandwich– and while traveling hundreds of miles home, nonetheless– he celebrated it as a point of pride. For Davorin, money was not only not an end in and of itself, it wasn't even necessarily a means to an end. It was a novelty. This man was born and raised in inarguable poverty, and by all empirical measures, he struck me as one of the wealthiest human beings I've ever even *heard of*, much more so, ever met in person.

Davorin's currency was his charm. It was his smile. It was his outward and explicit belief that everything would turn out alright so long as he never stopped believing in the magic of life. It was in his sincerest appreciation when he would look me in the eye each time I would hand him a smoke or some food, and he would cease chuckling for just a moment and thank me from his soul to mine. Sure, I can only imagine he had his days, like we all do, not perfectly graceful, not heroically courageous. It would be Pollyanna for me to assume otherwise. Even so, the Polaroid snippet I managed to snag from my few short hours in his presence is that of a King. He came from nothing and was going back to nothing, as far as one could measure from a strictly superficial perspective. Yet, not only did his disposition in the world not inhibit him from living each day to its absolute maximum, but his humbling origins would supercharge him with this prolific sense of playing with "house money." It was as if he knew damn well and at every fleeting moment that we're all going to die in the end and take nothing with us in the process, so fuck it! Put all the chips in the middle of the table, stare the menacing odds squarely in their ghastly face, and effortlessly laugh them to death.

That was it. Our time was over. As I went in to give him a hug and a cigarette for the wait of his connecting train, as fate would have it, a smoking-hot Italian girl closer to my age than his accidentally bumped into him as she passed by. He turned to make eye contact with her, and they both apologized to one another. He then turned and looked at me, winked, chuckled, and parted with, "Here we go…"

Just like that, those two walked off together: chatting, connecting, living. "Motherfucker!" I whispered to myself, watching this Hollywood-like continuation of his saga proceed without me– and with that bombshell in my stead. "Someday," I silently breathed through a tearful smile. I could only shake my head in disbelief. "Someday."

Third World Royalty: Part 2

In two blinks, I was back home from Europe. After roughly eight to nine weeks of living out of a backpack and on the rails, I was both out of money and out of emotional gas. I had managed to book a flight out of Paris a few weeks earlier than I had initially scheduled. The night I flew home coincidentally was the night that the infamous Hurricane Katrina made its notorious landfall in New Orleans. Of course, the existential turmoil in which I found myself twisting right then didn't hold a candle to the inferno of adversity those affected Southerners would go on to embrace for generations in the aftermath of that particular catastrophe. Even so, I will forever associate my internal storm, dishevelment, perplexity, lack of direction, and sense of "WHAT NEXT?" with that historical event. But at least I had a home to return to in Omaha and a crash pad where I could reconfigure a realistic expectation of what I would do with the rest of my life.

Living in Omaha was never exactly my forte. In hindsight, it was a divine place to be raised. It wasn't a megatropolis by any stretch, but it was also a far cry from being the commonly held misconception of a land chock full of cornfields and slackjawed twits. By and large, commonly agreed-upon moral values permeated the culture of my childhood, and some of the most salt-of-the-earth people I ever plan to meet originated there. Even so, I've never felt much of a soul connection to that land, nothing like Colorado or the greater American West. For whatever reason, the place of my childhood upbringing always did and seems like it always will give me some ineffable feeling of anxiety. I can't describe the feeling other than to say the idea of living in Omaha has always had this feel of a freezing, dreary November day listening to the sullenest of Simon and Garfunkle songs in a dark room. This imagery is precisely the subconscious schema that creeps its way into the sidecar of my stream of consciousness while contemplating my own hypothetically continued existence in that town.

The day I left for college, I inherently knew my best life lay somewhere in the ether out west. That I didn't magically marry a Dutch princess and live out my days in some sort of astronomically improbable existence in Europe didn't mean that I was packing it in and moving back home for good. Yuck– God, no! Indeed, I could slap together another quest, which perhaps wasn't quite as far-fetched as whatever Europe was supposed to be but also wasn't exactly the equivalent of me putting on the archetypal suit and tie and selling out to "The Man"– an *inconceivable* notion for young me.

After a few weeks back home, bored out of my mind, I decided moves had to be made, and I plain missed Colorado. It was early fall. The euphoric buzz of the Davorinesque rucksack life was long gone. I missed the mountains. I missed my college friends, most of whom were on the four-and-a-half to five-year slacker plan and were all gearing up for their final semester or two. Being in closer proximity to them seemed a logical starting point. God knows I was done with Ft. Collins and the idea of living in any college town, for that matter. I had outgrown the scene and needed to move on, seeing as how my uber-cerebral philosophy education had incinerated the scholastic faculties of my brain to a blackened char. But I knew I had to get back to Colorado in some capacity.

Not only did I make it back to Colorado, but I took it straight to the quintessential apex of Rocky Mountain living at its core. After contacting my stepsister, Holly, she convinced me to pack up my car and visit her at her remote mountain cabin outside Basalt. Where she lived was about an hour or so from the celebrated ski town of Aspen, and she was forcefully insistent that if there were ever a place for a young, fun-loving wildcard like myself to figure things out, that would be a Mecca.

Holly has never been one for being bashful or lazy. Rather than let me stay in her guest room for a couple of weeks and figure things out, she marched me to town on Day One and found me both a job and a place to live. Being a longtime real estate agent, mountain rescue EMT, and a touch of a socialite in the Roaring Fork Valley, it seemed as though Holly knew everyone around. She thrust me into the doors of a dynamite Italian restaurant, Bellissima. In lockstep with her pervasive personality, she was in with the G.M. and the bartenders, and she shooed me into a busser position they incidentally had to fill. As it would turn out, one of the bartenders was in with a CPA who was the CFO for a sushi joint in town and one of his backcountry ski buddies. The guy was looking for a roommate for his condo on the west side of town, off the roundabout. Holly drove me down there, and to her amazement, it was serendipitously the exact same condo that she lived in when she first moved to Aspen in the early 90s. The full circle was complete. I was home, I guess.

And it was settled. I would put my life as an existentialist on indefinite hold and potentially live out my days as a snowboarding, dope-smoking, womanizing, blue-collar, ski-town such-and-such. I was very much handed a lucrative job and a solid place to live in what is perhaps the most socially and culturally vaunted of all North American resort towns. What kind of damn fool would have balked at that setup straight out of undergrad? Even then, I knew deep down that it was not a place designed for someone of my nature to live out their days. Had I been born into unfettered wealth and money was never an issue, I would own property there as I write this. As that was never in my cards, Aspen would serve outstandingly as a cushy bridge between the idealistic, parentally-sponsored life of academia and the sobering reality of finally having to work for a living, pay my own way, and somehow, not hate my life in the process.

Getting fully established in town by mid-October was of paramount importance. Not only was I starting to get into a solid workflow during the waning offseason, but I made a few friends in short order. Brad was another busser at Bellissima and also was a recent college grad, though from my alma mater's sworn rival, CU at Boulder. It's not like I was ever douchey enough actually to rival someone from another school. Still, the graduates of that particular school have often been viewed as being very– ummmmm– "hit-and-miss" for your average beta State School graduate like me. Brad wasn't anything of the stereotype, and neither were his handful of college buddies, who also quickly became friends of my own.

October came and went. Thanksgiving arrived, and Ajax Mountain opened for business. Finally, I no longer would have to wake up at the asscrack of 4:30 AM, commute from Ft. Collins through the central Rocky Mountains I-70 corridor, and white-knuckle drive through the elements to get first tracks in the morning. I was never a crazy die-hard snowboarder by any standard ski-town measures. A minimum of 100 days on the mountain is considered the bottommost threshold for actual "bum status," and I'm sure my oppressive penchant for habitually sleeping in, in conjunction with my late-night working schedule, precluded my ability ever even to breech the 50s. I didn't care. I was afforded the ability to wake up whenever, jump on the mountain for at least a few top-to-bottom runs, and make it to work in time without any significant hustle– creature comforts.

On the morning of December 2, 2005, I woke up with an attitude. I won't even pretend to remember what it was about, only that I was feeling a bit chippy, and I naturally wanted to burn off my young man's angst with a most appropriately aggressive snowboard run down the mountain. It was snowing just a bit that morning, making for poor visibility, yet it produced only three or four inches of fresh powder from the night before. I was early that morning but didn't get first tracks. It appeared as if I had made the second or third rotation of enthusiasts, but there were untouched lines to be made, nevertheless.

Once I emerged at the top of the gondola, I flew. I cut lines as hard as my knees could stand. I whipped mindlessly around trees as though invincibility was a matter of sheer apathy. Not even halfway down the hill, I saw what is commonly referred to in bro culture as a "kicker," a smallish bump on the top of a measurable downslope. With minimal jumping experience on my board to speak of, I proceeded to launch off that thing as high as my angry legs could elevate me. If I didn't know better, I would say that I probably got a good six to eight feet in the air, didn't have the skill to get my board aimed straight downslope, couldn't determine the depth of the landing spot due to the visibility, and broke my tibia in multiple places thanks to the loose nature of my cheap snowboarding boots and inability to land the jump. Just like that, nine days into my first season living the boarder's life in Aspen, my year on the mountain was already shot.

By the time ski patrol tobogganed me to the bottom of the mountain, I was already a mess of tears. What started that morning as undefined angst had suddenly morphed into profound regret and unadulterated disappointment in myself. I allowed a cocktail of hubris, negativity, and testosterone to put me on the season-ending injured reserve.

What just days before was not far from the ultimate start to my post-college existence was just like that transformed into an ambulance ride to Aspen Valley Hospital; at least the attending EMT was one of Holly's best friends and my stalwart weed hookup, Michael Jackson. No, it was not *that* Michael Jackson, but another one. After Jacks dropped me off and they plastered up my leg with a fresh cast, I summoned a cab back to the condo and hobbled my way up the stairs, hauling the load of ski clothes, snowboard, crutches, painkillers, and self-disgust.

The ski season came and went. By April, I was well on my way through the thick of rehab and beyond ready to move on from the malaise of the previous winter. In May, once the dead of the off-season had passed, I returned to Bellissima to bus tables part-time, a physical impossibility since October. I had spent the past few months graduating back into the workforce, jockeying the front desk at one of the premier health clubs and spas in the Valley, Mountain High Life. At first, I despised the proposition, but my immobility rendered my possibilities minimal, and having to remain stationary to hold down the front of the house was the best of all opportunities. Once again, my employment was the byproduct of Holly knowing everyone in town.

Going through the motions of guest services at one of the most la-di-dah places of business in Aspen, Colorado, could not have been a much further cry from what I may have envisioned myself doing a year previous– having just finished up my four-year round-robin with Plato, Rousseau, Nietzsche, Kant, Frank Bacon, and company. Most of the regular patrons, townies mostly, were likable and fundamentally a carpe diem bunch of folks. They came off as highly educated, respectful, holistically well-balanced healthnuts 365 days a year and party hounds more like 350 or so. Nonetheless, every punch bowl is going to collect a few turds here and there, and sometimes, they would float right on over to the front desk of MHL.

I'd hate to overgeneralize, but a significant segment of the turd population appeared to be not the ultra, mega, or uber-wealthy, and certainly not the regular working-class who push the buttons and pull the levers to make the world go around. No, they were typically those residing a rung or two down the socioeconomic ladder of aristocracy, as some of them would certainly view it. A lot of those individuals, it would seem, frequently fell into the category of regular visitors to town– during peak seasons, of course. Often they would proceed to carry with them a vexing sense of entitlement based on their universally elite social standing, but this would seemingly collide with a competing sense of ruinous envy for those at the very zenith of the measuring stick. By all means, I do not want that to read as though a significant segment of second-home-owning, financially successful people fall anywhere near this demographic minority. It just so happens that if we had a hot mess diva chewing my ass over a less-than-superlative thermal mineral facial service, they, more often than not, were part of what I'll call the top 2%– not quite rolling with the 1's.

The most sterling case-in-point was Pamela Jordessy. She and her henpecked husband, Fleming, were the stereotypical assholes straight out of a Christopher Guest movie mocking the 2% on their Christmas and 4th of July vacations. In all honesty, Fleming wasn't terrible, but he would never say "please," "thank you," look any of us in the eye, or do anything more than grumble a request for the same locker key number that he received on his last visit. If another member were using that particular key at the moment, he would take the next locker of numerical succession and stomp off down the hall, cussing life under his breath. I have no idea what he did for a living, but he looked like he had spent 70-80 hours a week for the last 40 years funding this miserable existence of broken, petty expectations. Plus, he was married to Pamela.

Pamela Jordessy– God forbid there is ever more than one– will forever serve as the prototype of "Karen"– the unmistakable American bitch. She was not just a regular at the club when she would come in on her quarterly/semi-annual visits, but she would be there all day and every day of their getaway. In a place that couldn't be set anymore in the heart of the majestic Rocky Mountains, she would insist on spending almost all daylight hours indoors at the club getting the complete Saudi Princess treatment. Her days typically started with an 80-minute deep tissue massage with the same young stud masseuse, Blaine– (I'd hate to think why only him– gross). After that, she would most likely go in for a body wrap, followed by a facial, pedicure, manicure, and two hours of God-knows-what in the ladies' locker room.

She always had at her side her immaculately groomed Toy Maltese named Charleston. I would never harbor a grudge against an animal for any conceivable reason. I unconditionally love them, and nothing they do can possibly be judged through the lens of a self-contemplating human. That said, I hated Charleston's little doggie guts. He was sweet and not yippy whatsoever, a trait that I often find deal-breaking in my outright ability to love tiny dogs. But poor Charleston became a mascot for us. As previously noted, not only was he forever presumably within somewhere between $1000 weekly grooming services, but he was always outfitted in a toy-dog-sized collared shirt, perfectly color coordinated with a matching diamond-studded collar. His labels would reflect the extravagances of Louis Vuitton, Coco Channel, Burberry, Brooks Brothers, and Ralph Lauren, just to name a few. Yet, my disdain wasn't rooted in the fact that this butt-sniffing creature at any given time had on clothing more expensive than the composite value of my entire lifetime's adult wardrobe. The hate emerged because whenever Pamela would come to check out from the day's services, she would almost exclusively talk to us using Charleston as her disappointed customer comfort doll– a ventriloquist dummy reminiscent of what children are instructed to use for demonstrations in courtroom settings.

Rather than outright complain that the temperature of her facial exfoliants felt four degrees cooler than usual, she would strap on the fakest smile that a face operated upon no less than a dozen times can convey, look straight at Charleston as she propped him up on the counter, and proceeded to bounce him up and down, puppeteering him in sync with her high-pitched dog voice impersonation: "Gee, Pamela, it sure was another great day at Mountain High Life, except for______________." She would go on to list a few minor complaints in this voice, but when she started to get worked up, she would softly let

Charleston back down on the counter, look whichever one of us lucky shlubs in the face, and go off on any given tangent, typically with an increasingly angry tone of voice and a demand for her (near) daily chat with the Guest Services Manager, Elizabeth. She was a hardline 15% tipper. In Blaine's case, *he* was most likely the one "hardline tipping" *her*, one can only suppose– gross.

If I were to have experienced her in all of her glory once, maybe even twice, I would have been utterly appalled. In the wake of my education, firmly entrenched in the pursuit of intrinsic moral value, this woman was a world-renowned affront to every last virtue known to the history of ethics. Fortunately, I witnessed this enough to appreciate the novelty and privilege of watching this cinematic mockumentary of someone living out the hyperbolic reality of what achieving the conventional idea of the American Dream can look like in its most toxic version. Between Fleming, Charleston, and Pamela, I was afforded a grievous peek into the window of what the cosmically damning world of wealth, eccentricity, superficial preoccupations, and ungrounded expectations may become when left to the chemistry of nature. It reeked of being equal parts depressing, frightening, tragic, and pathetic.

The flip side of the coin of stereotypes, which I was happy to find as being predominantly the case during my Aspen experience, was finding that almost every celebrity, professional athlete, political figure, or any other world-recognized entity that I had the pleasure of serving between those two jobs acted as unassumingly, unentitled, charitable, appreciative, and outright friendly as one could hope to serve. I'm not sure if I was just lucky or if there is something to being of ubiquitous stardom and having a place like Aspen to vacate, where the professionals of the service industry are rare to resort to fan-boy-level behavior. At any rate, it was a pleasant surprise peeling back the layman-perceived veil of mystery to find this morally satisfying phenomenon well at play.

The one celeb who didn't seem to shine his love all over me shall remain nameless, but let's qualify his A-lister status by saying that he was in one of the indispensably classic American mobster movies, his stage name in which, would be immediately recognizable to any 20th-century movie buff. He wasn't a creep but a bit brash. Although his face was traditionally of a household variety, the few years leading up to the encounter must have been pretty rough. Instead of recognizing the face of an aged heartthrob, I only looked up from the check-in desk one day to see some leathery-skinned old guy throwing a guest pass in my direction and heedlessly trying to take off down the hall and to the gym floor. As an order of protocol, I stopped him in his tracks and insisted there was simply no way I could allow him to work out in the club without first signing a liability waiver. He begrudgingly returned to the desk, quickly scribbled some nonsense across the agreement's wording, and hustled back towards his workout.

As it wasn't all that uncommon of an occurrence, I didn't think much of it. I grabbed the signed form, filed it away, and went back about my business of downtime work. Not a few seconds after the interface, my coworker Terry walked over to me and, with a big smile, just stared me down and said something like, "Really, dude? Did you really just shakedown XXXXXXXXX (famous stage name) for a signature?"

Wait, what? "What do you mean, XXXXXXXXX? That old fart? That wasn't XXXXXXXXX."

Not feeling overly confident with my reactive assertion, I walked down the hall and looked at the gym floor. It was, indeed, XXXXXXXXX. Yikes. I guess the moral of the story was less scotch and more sleep. Stardom had him looking like a racehorse "rode hard and put away wet" one too many times.

And then there was the Edward Abbey guy. It pains me that I can't remember his name to save my life. Anyhow, after maybe a year or so of working the front desk, I would drive the club's complimentary shuttle within town periodically. Not just being a sporadic break away from having to manage the bitchfactor up front, I could also get a chance to make a few cash tips here and there and sometimes perhaps stop by my place in town and smoke cigarettes on the clock. What a country!

Well, one snowy night, I was transporting some older gentleman from the club to the timeshare he was staying at by Clark's Market. I'm not sure exactly how we got on the subject. Still, at some point, we established that Edward Abbey, the famous literary defender of the Western American wilderness– not to mention one of my all-time favorite writers and folk heroes– was, by his account, one of this guy's best friends back in the day. Forget the movie stars and politicians. This was a once-in-a-lifetime ten-minute shuttle ride for me. In that short amount of time, I assaulted him with a bare minimum of a dozen concrete questions about Abbey and, more specifically, his legendary burial.

The going myth was that Edward Abbey was so in love with the red rocks of Utah that a couple of his buddies were rumored to have hiked his shrouded corpse out into the vast wilderness of the Maze District of Canyonlands National Park, and they buried him anonymously in an unmarked grave. This character went on not only to confirm the suspicion but also to inform me that he was one of the hikers and that they left a cryptic placard engraved on stone saying something to the effect that the legendary Edward Abbey was buried within a reasonable vicinity of the sign and that his presence would be forever one with the Utah desert and greater American West– a detail satisfyingly befitting my romantically-principled muse.

However, the "old guard" ZG crowd was the best of the bunch. "ZG" refers to the first two letters on the Colorado license plates, once uniformly attributed to any vehicle registered in Pitkin County (Greater Aspen). Over the years, the swelling population of the area would render this licensing process obsolete. Still, the original residents would be grandfathered into the old coding system for as long as they were to reside in the valley. This distinction would denote an era when the town's name was not synonymous with galavanting in excess. Way before becoming shorthand for haute couture activewear and apres ski happy hours, the place was by all accounts much more folksy, funky, and wild. Look it up. Hunter S. Thompson, a legend of the valley and longtime resident of Woody Creek, once upon a time ran for Pitkin County Sheriff leveraging hot-button stances like needing to repave the streets with sod, setting up stocks and a whipping post on the courthouse lawn for publicly punishing dishonest drug dealers—the ones of better business practices notwithstanding— and renaming Aspen to "Fat City."

The ZGs were typically those who had bought property in the area in the 1970s or before and, as such, were of an aged minority residing in alpine paradise at an honest cost of living. Deduce what you will, but this niche demographic seemed to host some of Aspen's most zenlike and well-balanced individuals. Of this bunch, the postergrandpa was an aged stud named Barry Brood. His last name could not have been less indicative of his overall zest for life. Barry was in his early eighties and gassed up with the energy of someone less than half of his age. You could tell when he would shuffle up the sidewalk and into the club's front doors that the physical toll of the years had their effect on his thin, elderly frame. Each time he'd come in, he'd effectively announce himself by softly whistling or quietly singing, in the raspiest of old-guy pitches, some tune that was without fail written and initially performed in the 1940s or '50s.

Barry bought land in Aspen in the early 60s and spent three decades in the roads department as a personnel manager for various construction projects in the greater Glenwood Springs I-70 corridor. Evidently, he had done well for himself but was not by any stretch rolling with the "Aspen Jonses." As he would often note, there's no way he could have built this life for himself on his civil salary had he started right there and then, the place where he found us serving the masses.

He was grateful. He was insightful. He would come in at least five days every week, and each time, he would spend anywhere from two to ten minutes chatting up the "help" at the front desk. To him, we were anything but help. He looked each of us flush in the eyes, asked our stories, laughed our joys, and bemoaned our struggles. He knew us as well as any given one of us would be willing to let him in. Sure, I would periodically see him on the gym floor, walking the treadmill at a moderate pace or lounging post-steam in the men's locker room, old wrinkled balls shamelessly peeking from his towel as he regaled the other codgers with self-deprecating anecdotes about aging and mortality.

But it felt like he lived to commiserate with the aspiring youth in their daily professional baptisms by fire at the front desk. He knew our names, and he understood our dispositions. He embraced our struggles. He bathed us in hope. Because of this, Barry indelibly remains one of my lifelong role models for maturing into old age with class, charm, and humility.

That first year in Aspen was a mixed bag for sure. Primarily, I had reasoned to believe that I had cultivated a somewhat novel and exceedingly comfortable existence. Once I was fully rehabbed and out enjoying the boundless, rugged offerings up and down Independence Pass– hiking, camping, exploring– the appeal of living out one's existence in such a geo-locale made perfect sense. It had all the rustic makings of what I spent my college life doing on weekends. Yet, it was cultured, educated, encouraged a physically active lifestyle, and had a party scene that rivaled any I had experienced in a notably fun four years of college. Best yet, it had a nearly 50/50 guy-to-girl ratio. The last factoid was borderline insane compared to just about any other ski town in North America. During those years, I remember reading the rankings in Colorado alone, and most resort areas in Summit County (Keystone, Breckenridge, A-Basin, etc.) had ratios ranging from 10:1 to 50:1. Woof! One might as well sign up for Seminary.

When almost a full year had passed, not only was I spending most of my working hours at Bellissima, but I was somehow promoted to waiter. It wasn't as much of a promotion as an off-season assignment, which fell my way by default. The veteran seasonal servers didn't usually take their hours back until early December, and I got to cut my teeth at that pay grade during the deader months of the fall. My journey from busser to server had its bumps and bruises. Over a few months, I would polish the edges of my craft to a point where I could get things done accurately and with a focused hustle. Yet, projecting the professional attitude of someone being more at play than at work was a battle that became increasingly more difficult to fight. I was fully physically healed, inundated with my outdoor undertakings, making more money at the restaurant and the club, and my social life was perfectly apt. Even so, the days felt like they were growing darker and not simply because we were well past the autumnal equinox and on our way to solstice. I couldn't help but feel depressed and in need of something, but what was going on, I was not too sure.

My most extraordinary daily reprieve was engaging a particular cold-bar kitchen worker at Bellisima. His real name was Guillermo, but he insisted on going by "Antonio"– I have no idea why. Antonio was a legally-carded migrant worker from San Salvador. Much like the majority of the Hispanic working populace of Aspen, he would commute daily about an hour each way (two in the winter) from Glenwood Springs and spend no fewer than 12 hours per workday prepping and assembling cold items (salad components, desserts, charcuterie, etc.). He would do so as though he was one of Snow White's whistling dwarves.

Antonio could not have stood a hair above five feet tall and wasn't portly but had softly rounded features and a pencil-thin mustache, permanently fixed as a semi-circle complement to his gleefully smiling face. He told me he was 33, but Antonio legitimately looked like he might have finished puberty 20 minutes before any given work shift. His incredulously youthful glow was in sheer defiance of the reality of his life's disposition on this planet.

As he would inform me during a few months' time, he fought to get a working visa a few years prior, extricating himself from a veritable war zone of narco-based activity. Tragically for him, he was forced to make this journey without his wife or three children in tow. His endgame was to spend 100% of every earned dime between feeding his family from afar and lobbying (bribing) Salvadoran officials for his family's priority in the emigration process. Unlike me, his lesser wages weren't funding season ski passes, cannabis, or drinks for the ladies after work. He was financing the dreams of a lionhearted migrant worker and family man.

Each time I would go to pick up a Caesar salad or tiramisu, he would make a point to stop in the middle of the pandemonium, as though he heard the storied Buddhist Mindfulness Bell, look at me, and with a thumbs up cheerfully question me, "¿¡Chingón Chingón!?" As he would explain to me, "Chingón" is Spanish for "cool" or "awesome."

Even though each time I would be presented with this ritual of his, I was progressively and internally a touch darker than the time before. I would do my best to reply with my privileged-yet-melancholy-white-guy's forced version of "¡Chingón Chingón!" I loved Antonio. I never wanted to dump water on his fire. I was in permanent awe and reverence for his backstory of ultimate triumph. He was an animated anthem to the glory of Dios. His resilience was an aberration of the Universal Game of Strife. He was not precisely Davorin, but if I didn't know better, I'd say they hailed from that same sacred neighborhood of the universe– the overlooked, impoverished slums of Nirvana.

I wished I could steal his mojo. I yearned to bottle him up into a capsule and chase him with a glass of Sangiovese, allowing myself to smile away the unnameable discomfort slowly taking over my jaded, commonplace outlook on life. By all empirical life measures, my worst day would have been his grandest ¡Chingón! ¡Chingón! His best day might have stoned me dead in my tracks. It was an irony that wasn't remotely lost on me, particularly as we lived it out in the moment.

Antonio became a Buddhalike effigy for me in that frenetic space of Bellissima's chic, glitzy, trendy, and vapid universe. He couldn't recognize a celebrity or world leader to save his life. He was second lowest on the kitchen totem pole, ranking just before the dishwasher. He was practically invisible to most patrons as they walked in the front doors, despite his cold bar and smiling face being the first thing in the line of sight past the hostess stand. The rich. The famous. The decadent, sexy, happening, pulsating crowds of town would pass him by on the way in and on the way out. They would relish his salads and cold cuts and gush over his desserts. Yet, I can't imagine even one of them ever knew the true magnificence of the elbow they just happened to brush by. He was a God among amoeba (myself included), though a God who still wouldn't be enough to save me from what was coming.

A reckoning with fate was brewing, and I was about to enter a reality no one should *ever* have to imagine. Not the legacy of Davorin nor that of Antonio could prepare me for what came next.

Black Tuesday

Tuesday, October 17, 2006, began as any other day in my newer Aspen life. It had been just over a year since I pieced my existence together to become a novice outdoorsman and customer serviceman of multiple hats and faces. Always having been a creature of habit, my weeks took on a comforting predictability of Tuesday and Friday mornings holding down the front of the club, accompanied by Thursday through Sunday nights feeding the hungry masses at Bellissima. I partied a few nights a week, hiked as much as the muddy season would allow, and even reestablished a habit of going to the gym at the club, a practice I hadn't regularly maintained since a stint during my senior year of high school.

It was a punishingly slow day at the club. Our few patrons were the regular townies, contentedly proceeding about their leisurely off-season routines. Seeing as there were no visitors to town, the shuttle service wasn't up and running. After having completed almost every conceivable downtime task I was expected to perform, I managed to break the monotony by assuming the project of driving around town, picking up fallen branches of aspen trees, complete with adjoining yellowed leaves, all to be added to the ambiance of the front window display of the club. A novel task indeed, I milked the clock as long as I could, roaming the club shuttle around town, soaking in the crisp alpine air in one breath, exhaling the smokey billows of my cherried cigarette with the next. Octobers in the Rockies are sacred in all their autumn-like glory, and this fall day had all of the classical hallmarks of such. Gold. Green. Cool. Quiet. Effortless. Beautiful.

By two o'clock, I was off work and home within minutes. True to my creaturely habit of post-shift rituals, I loaded my bubbler, burnt my offerings to the cannabis gods, and walked back into my bedroom from the conveniently attached outdoor balcony. My cell phone buzzed away in my pocket a second or two later. I pulled it out and, across the screen, read my brother's name. He and I have traditionally been close, and even though we didn't have any highly established communication habits, it seemed obtrusively out of place for him to call me on a Tuesday mid-afternoon.

"Hey man, what's up?" I answered.

"Zachary, I need you to sit down," his shaken voice would fumble– those seven words paralyzing me in place. Although they had yet to ever apply to my situation, I knew those words and the magnitude of what they traditionally were used to preface. Instinctively, I fell backward onto the mattress of my bed, all four of my limbs instantaneously devoid of all blood flow.

"What do you mean?" I reflexively retorted.

"I need you to sit down right now," his voice graduated from shaken to outright disturbed and authoritative. "Dad's dead," – ruptured the thunderclap through the receiver of the phone.

The rest is a blur, as they say– a primitively hysterical, screaming, raging, quivering, hyperventilating, visceral, quasi-catatonic blur. It was the statement that would irretrievably cast to the annals of history everything I once believed I knew. With two seismic syllables, my older brother had ripped away whatever curtain of youthful ignorance I was ever indulged regarding the generational darkness that would eventually take our father from himself, from us.

Much like his mother before him, my father, Shelly (no middle name) Perelman, decided that he had endured one too many of life's oppressive trials, and he successfully chose to end his own life. He was 61 years old, my unequivocal hero, role model, and best friend, and he picked that dreary day in his suburban Detroit bedroom to leave all of it behind, including me.

There is no word in the human Zeitgeist for the sensation one feels when the world around a person is pulverized into an infinitely ruinous mountain of rubble– the grief of losing a loved one to suicide. Black and white become one and the same. Gravity ceases. Motion freezes. Green is brown, and one plus one doesn't mathematically equal anything. It's the complete and utter cessation of everything remotely decent about the human experience. If "oblivion" and "despair" were to have a child, and that child was to be raised by "torment" in the very depths of Satan's fiery hellscape, then this profane masterpiece would be its magnum opus.

The blur continued. After several manic phone calls among my family members, my mother summoned Holly to pick me up from my condo and drive me back to Basalt to spend the night at her place. I said virtually nothing to anyone for hours and hours on end. I might have slept that night. I might not have. A semi-conscious fog would see me from sunset through to sunrise, an animate corpse subsisting through the darkest of nights. When the morning broke in full, she would wrangle together my grief-drunk impression of a person and drive me an hour and a half to the Eagle County Regional Airport, where I would sob at the gate for an hour, awaiting my flight to Denver and ultimately to Omaha, where his body would be laid to rest.

Accurate to my mental schema of the town and in perfectly appropriate accordance with the morbidity of the situation, Omaha was a cold, dreary, melancholy void. The funeral drew a few dozen mourners, a small fraction of the people whose hearts my father doubtlessly moved in one way or another over the years. Within two hours, all three of his children would publicly condemn his final act while simultaneously reconfiguring the effect of his now-polarizing legacy of creating the Ultimate Void for us all. Shovelful by shovelful of dirt, we cast upon the pine box as the casket slowly lowered into the fissure of earth below. The grave was a standard six to eight feet deep, but it might as well have been the black hole of a collapsed supernova—the negative space of which would mercilessly steal what little spirit remained in us each. No cubic amount of soil would ever wholly fill the void.

Once buried, the proper mourning and reconfiguration of reality began. Concepts of the simplest, most complex, and everything in between were to be redefined– each one, now in the context that my father, best friend, and hero was not only gone, but he was gone of his own choosing. He effectively met his match. All the lessons of perseverance, every moment of positive reinforcement, paternal belief, and investment in my being were all demarcated by a nature that had become arguably null and void. The champion joined the ranks of the vanquished. In time, the seethingly obvious tenets of existence (e.g., $1+1=2$, and night is not day) would regain their intuitively believable essences. Yet, the world in which they permeate their meanings had dissolved into a murky broth of "Who fucking cares?" My valiant leader was gone, and he was never coming back– a decision of his own making.

As the universe would appropriately see to it, my voyage back to Aspen was almost as physically taxing as my world had become emotionally uninhabitable. After about a half-hour into my flight back to Denver– my connection to the Aspen Regional Airport– I defied the FAA mandate to stay seated with my belt fastened, and I sprinted to the airplane bathroom. I wouldn't come out again until about 15 minutes left on the flight. At some point in the past few grief-stricken days, my body's immunity defenses succumbed to the stress, and I had been spawned a puking, shitting, flu-ravaged, fatherless cadaver of misery incarnate.

When I arrived at DIA to await my commuter flight back to the mountains, I set up shop in one of the bathroom stalls. I proceeded to live out a contest of woe: physical intestinal distress versus the prospect of living another eight-plus decades without seeing my father's face or hearing his voice even once more. Had there been a magic button for me to press at that very moment in the airport bathroom, one which would forever whisk me away to a world of no more pain or loss or existential torment, one also devoid of all joys and all other loved ones, I would not have hesitated to push it for a moment. Whether he would have been waiting for me on the other side was of little consequence.

The totality of the pain, physical and emotional, was unequivocally the most insurmountable brew of affliction I would never wish upon another human, no matter how non-sympathizable they may happen to be. Non-being seemed to be a divine proposition to the alternative. Pond scum should never endure such torture.

In the following weeks and months, I would gradually begin to go back through the motions of life. Of course, nothing was ever the same, and a cloudy lens of sorrow filtered every moment through its diminished spectrum of light. Everything was a conscious effort. The untouchable comforts of the immutable past and the harrowing possibilities of the monochrome future would engage in an endless shoving match, using me as their mutual battering ram. And this paradoxical ebb and flow would mysteriously suspend me in a constant zenlike moment of pure being. The pureness may have been of a soulless, numbing, and seemingly meaningless state of existence, but it was whole, pristine, and a force of immovable proportions. The climb back to everyday life was a slow ascent– one foot forward, then the next.

I would return to work about six or eight weeks after the fact. Management at the restaurant and the club were each overwhelmingly supportive and thoughtful in giving me all the time and resources needed to return to a place where I could even go through an impersonation of employment. I'll never forget the GM of the restaurant, Thom Edinburgh– a guy who previously struck me as a pretty-boy, too-cool-for-school parody of an '80s ski-town blowhard– insisted on taking me out to sushi before I was even remotely ready to come back to work. We sat in awkward silence for the first three-quarters of the meal, and I hardly ate any of my bento box. I don't know that I even felt marginally better about my life's disposition after that outing. Still, I do recall being moved to humility, my realizing that the previous iteration of me (life before the suicide) couldn't have been more wrong about Thom. He may have lacked the ability to communicate with a bereaved employee interpersonally. Still, he eclipsed this one-thousandfold with his mere presence and ability to accompany the strain of my deafening silence.

Within three or four months, I was mostly back to functional form. Because the A-team servers at the restaurant were back for the winter season, I was naturally demoted, not to busser, but a single step down to food runner. It was a touch less pay than bussing but half as time-consuming and infinitely less humbling than humping dirty dishes back to the dishwasher all night. The front desk at the club welcomed me back with the warmest and most open of arms, and they didn't even put me on spa reservations for a few weeks, which was indubitably the most annoying of all guest service duties. Simply checking people in and handing out locker room keys proved a cathartic exercise in essential productivity. I didn't know how crucial it would be until it happened, but receiving the condolences and support of my regular patrons, much like Barry Brood, would somehow elevate my beleaguered spirit, much like rising tides presenting a messy barge of floating rubbish closer to the shine of the enduring sun. Suddenly, some of the served became my servers. Slowly but certainly, the devastation of the wildfire had sown its seeds of rebirth, and a lifetime of regrowth had commenced. The forest was far from established, but at least the blaze had cracked open the fortressed embryos of new life, gifting future flora to my charcoal-ravaged, earthen floor.

However, the ascent back was anything but perfectly linear. Despite my ability to be baseline serviceable at work, I was still a shell of my former hospitable self. One day, when I was busily running the shuttle service for the club, I got a request for a pickup of a spa patron in Starwood. The problem was that the shuttle's service wasn't to run further than the far west roundabout in town, and with good reason.

Starwood was a good 15-20 minutes past the specified limit. With one shuttle to service the entire clientele of the club, leaving the designated zone would indisputably put me out of commission for over a half hour, destroying my capacity to make tips as well as expediently move masses of people around town in ten minutes or less. From a utilitarian perspective, it was a rock-stupid proposition. Serve one person at the inconvenience of ten.

Well, because a newer employee errantly offered my services to pick up in Starwood, I was conscripted to the task. When I got out to pick up the patron, things started cordially. She seemed pleasant enough, and anyone picked up in Starwood would likely have a loose $20 or $50 to throw an Aspen service worker. Over the course of the prolonged 20-minute ride, I did my best to make small talk and kindly explain to her that the shuttle service was not supposed to go past the roundabout; picking her up where I did was a one-off exception to the rule. It was a hectic day at the club, and I wouldn't have the ability to give her a complimentary ride back home. She said she understood, but clearly she didn't. I should have known she sucked when I dropped her off at the club, and she outright stiffed me on a tip.

It was about two hours later when I was on the far side of town, dropping off my latest patron, and I got a call from the front desk telling me that I had a patron waiting for me and that she was not being overly patient. When I pulled back into the club parking lot, out strolled the Starwood starlet, nonchalantly sliding into the backseat of the van as though we had never met.

"Starwood, please," she casually blurted.

"Ma'am, I do apologize, but I thought we were clear on my inability to take you over a half hour out of the designated shuttle zo...," I began to reexplain when I was abruptly cut off. I couldn't even begin to tell you what her response was exactly, but it was loud, charged, and fundamentally reactive. She fastened her seatbelt, dug in her claws, and insisted on her free ride home. The first five or ten minutes of the ride was a ping pong match– my repeated servings of reason systematically returned with backhands of unfounded entitlement. By the time the shuttle proceeded well past the roundabout, all customer service decorum had been abandoned and done so with reckless fervor.

I distinctly recall lobbing phrases like "boo-fucking-hoo," "cry me a river," and "useless, former-trophy wife" with liberating ease. Absolutely dismayed by my unfiltered honesty, she threatened to call my manager immediately after she got home and said that I would be sorry. As though I had just finished watching the movie *Bad Santa*, I threw the classic Billy Bob Thornton line at her verbatim, "You think you can make my life any worse?? Take your best *fucking* shot!" Except, I wasn't laughing, and it felt like the most authentic statement I could possibly hurl at this diva in the relative aftermath of my father's suicide. When we pulled into her driveway, she pulled out a single dollar bill and put it in my tip jar. She threw one more insult at me and quickly slammed the door behind her. My biggest immediate regret was not having the reaction time to crumble up the pathetic George Washington note and throw it in her face before the door abruptly closed. She never called my manager. Perhaps she actually felt my misery.

The climb back to a liveable life couldn't have been more tedious, and it couldn't have been more assertive. But the glacial pace of learning to live once again had been unchangeably cast into motion. Life would insist on itself and proceed in its perpetual forward fashion, my begrudging it or not. The slow creep of the darkness I had felt in the months leading up to my father's suicide had been savagely exposed. It was such an unfathomable notion that I refused to see it for what it was when it arose, that first year out of college. I was genetically predisposed to clinical depression, and his final act of violence would surgically pinpoint this malady with my own, increasing sense of unreasonable helplessness. I would never go as far as to say that I had ever actually contemplated a methodology to carry out my demise. Yet, I would be lying through my teeth if I were to proclaim that hypothetically fantasizing about my own, premature death was not a notion that would habitually give a comforting reprieve to the nagging reality of the unavoidable agonies of this life.

With his unforgivable act, I was, for all practical purposes, saved from the fatally suggestive inclinations of my clinically-depressed, unmedicated, inner thoughts. To this day, I will insist that if he hadn't done it to himself, there is a genuine possibility that I would have opened Pandora's box for the beloved characters in my life. I've been on anti-depressants ever since.

This is not a sour grapes rationalization. This is the purely factual deduction of cause and effect. Had my father not completed that incredibly selfish act, he might have left his son to actualize the same unimaginable destruction of his own making. Ironically enough, his ultimate act of selfishness saved me from perpetrating that of my very own. With this morbid gift of his, I have tethered myself to making one unnegotiable commitment of my own in this life– never follow his lead. Even though the more significant swathe of my life has proven itself me-focused, I can't ever imagine scorching the earth around me in such a way, yielding it a sterile wasteland for the survivors of my deed.

That my omni-loving father found this a feasible out simply stands as a testament to how unbearable his reality must have become. For this reason, and this reason alone, I will never fully condemn his self-elected exit from our lives. What final sensation drove him to manufacture a rambling, listless, and logically nonsensical suicide note, leave it for his stepwife to find at the bottom of the stairs of his house (imploring her to call the police and not walk upstairs herself– something she tragically did anyhow), and ultimately fasten a self-fashioned noose around his neck, was a phenomenon beyond any mentally healthy human's ability to comprehend. Global nuclear warfare couldn't manufacture such a boundless space of universal havoc. My sage was forever gone and relegated to infinity with a desperation unknown to any living being of sustained existence. His struggle as a man on this earth and in this lifetime simply conquered his remaining life force. He gave us everything he had to offer until all that was left to give was his emotionally anemic body, abandoned by faith, reason, proper dopamine/serotonin levels, and the eternal flame of hope.

Not only did my father fail my father, but I would go on to argue that existence itself failed my father. His parents were typical of their generation, dutiful but stoic and pragmatic. At the time, they were, by all standard measures, considered a good and wholesome family. No one was abused. Everyone was fed, clothed, educated, and reasonably well supported financially and practically. Even so, he lived in a house where his parents ranked their affection toward their kids, and regular mantras of "I love you" were seldom spoken. My grandparents didn't even bother giving him a middle name, for Christ's sake. The approach couldn't have been less like the lives he (and my mother) would someday go on lovingly to provide for his three children. Over 17 years later, I'm still trying to forgive my grandparents for their shortcomings as parents to my father. I consciously have to remind myself that they were given incomplete parents themselves, and to compare them to my dad wouldn't be overly fair. Unlike them, something deep within him was strong enough to break the cycle and learn to openly and actively express unconditional love for his kids.

My father was far from a perfect person. He had his foibles and follies, as we all do. But he was my father. He was honest and decent. He was outwardly folksy and kind to perfect strangers. He often had the perfect anecdote of wisdom just waiting for its chance to lighten the world around him. He was funny, handsome, and downright attractive in the most virtuous of ways. People naturally gravitated toward him. When he was all there– the months leading up to his suicide notwithstanding– he was a sheer beacon of light. And this is how I choose to remember him. He will always be my beacon. And as the years go by, I'm relieved to say that its glow has rebounded to a luminous luster, though of a much different hue from that of its original self.

California Gleaning Part : 1

By the late summer of 2008, I had developed a peculiar sensation of stir craziness. As one might intuit, the confluence of my father's death, my manifest dissatisfaction with serving tables and placating spa divas, as well as my growing social claustrophobia of living in a town of 6,000 full-time residents ultimately drove me from whatever comfort zone I had established for myself and back out into the enigmatic backcountry of the unknown. Unlike my collegiately accrued anxiety– inherently begotten via my formal philosophy education and which endlessly fueled my quixotic European adventures– this particular feeling of unease lent no helpful suggestions as to how its accompanying demons were to be adequately exorcised. I didn't have any inkling as to what was next. I knew I was over my jobs. I was over living in a rundown, ramshackle condo with four other bachelors– a proposition on par with living among the uncleanliest and noisiest of God's civilized beasts. Much like the impetuous young man I once was, I acted and then planned.

My action? I purchased a one-way ticket to Bangkok, Thailand. With a mere couple of thousand bucks to my name, I spontaneously and without rationale decided that getting my vaccinations and a plane ticket to Asia would be the next chapter in this memoir. And why not? I hated the totality of my existence. My jobs were shit. My old man and hero was dead– and by his choosing, nonetheless. There were no more female or outdoor adventure distractions left with which I could mask my life's paramount shortcomings. Asia was far away. It was reportedly cheap and relatively easy to travel improvisationally. The women were gorgeous. The food looked even better. Maybe I could find that under-the-table job or unicorn of a princess– those elusive European fantasies of mine– but this time, *actually* waiting for me in *these* exotic lands. Ya. That must have been it.

My well-wishers and everyday acquaintances applauded my drastic approach. They saw an individual unhappy with the conventional and willing to scrap it all to swing for the fences and will into existence the radical changes I so desperately yearned to actualize. It all flew in the face of common wisdom, and my actions mirrored those of a wholly present and fundamentally fearless individual. I was openly apprehensive about making such monumental life changes, and my willful vulnerability on the matter was as much of a subconscious attempt to get me to believe in my uncalculated actions as the person I was explaining them to. In all reality, I was sad. I was lost. I was running. I was avoiding my most authentic self, and I was looking for a place of numbness– where loss, disappointment, expectation, potential, vocation, purpose, identity, virtue, altruism, love, or anything of the like were as futile and fleeting as a fart in a dust storm.

My family wasn't having it. I vaguely recall that my brother was relatively mum on my whole approach. I don't remember any static from him. However, I also can't recall any semblance of support, a somewhat indicting omission from my memory, as he has always been one of my most prominent advocates. My sister outright shut me down when I asked to borrow some money for my voyage, and in retrospect, I'm so glad she did. Knowing damn well I had zero plan or directive and that we were all still very much existentially disheveled– even two years after my dad's death– she called me out for my protracted willingness for denialism and the unaccountability I was increasingly demonstrating with my haphazard life choices. I had no idea what I was doing, and she knew it as simple as the fact that water is wet.

My mom was even more outspoken in her disagreement with my plan, or lack thereof. For all of the frilly romanticism, contrived fearlessness, and whimsical tendencies I witnessed and ultimately absorbed from my manically-spirited father, I was thankfully balanced out by a mother grounded in a world of responsibility, reason, prudence, and temperance. At the time, these overriding virtues of my mother infuriated the broken and rudderless child I still had residing deep within. The little boy who will always be figuratively standing on the front porch– waiting for the inspirational yet tactfully unsubstantial archetype of my dad to come home– hated that my one remaining parent was the one with too much bedrock of sensible character to indulge my deluded fantasies. Indeed, had that inscrutably perfect role model of mine been there– the naively conjured fantasy of my once-hero father– I would have gotten full blessing for my foolhardy journey to exotic distractions. Yet, the living parent I had left to appeal to was not the hapless dreamer. She was not the illogical pushover. She stood firm and outspoken in her defiance of the moves I was making, and we even got into a verbal altercation over the matter. I'm incredibly thankful that, to this day, this is one of my only memories of arguing with my mom.

It was Thanksgiving of 2008. I had already bounced from Aspen, stashing a few boxes of this and that in Holly's basement, and was temporarily living out the last couple of weeks in the country back home in Omaha. With my ticket (digitally) in hand, the requisite vaccines coursing through my veins, my backpack and its necessary contents packed, and one week until my departure, I was barely hanging on. I would mentally pace myself in circles to the end of each day among waves of sheer anxiety. Everything was unfolding according to whatever guise of a plan I had made, and the opportunity to begin again had drawn closer at a woefully sluggish pace.

And then, that very day, the citizens of Thailand decided that they'd had enough of their broken governmental structure and engaged in a junta. Just like that, the Grand Palace of Thailand was overrun with violent protests. All air travel to the country was forced into a suspension, which would go on for weeks. My ticket was voided and refunded. My elaborately aimless diversionary tactic of having to face the rest of my (constructive) life was thwarted. The universe would see that my destructively fantastical pursuit was shot dead in its tracks.

I was so pissed I recused myself from Thanksgiving dinner, an unheard-of and since-unreplicated act of me toothlessly protesting the tides of fate.

FUCK!!

To my dismay and my family's delight, I was forced back to the drawing board.

One thing was clear. I couldn't stay in Omaha. As previously noted, I knew the day I left for college that I would never permanently hang my hat in the Midwest ever again. Naturally, I was giddy with the need to pack up my car and head westward on I-80, but Colorado wasn't an option. I needed something bold and new after four years in Ft. Collins and three years in Aspen. Following a week or two of scouring the internet for compelling opportunities out west, I discovered that Northern Arizona University in Flagstaff was offering a 12-day intensive for a Wilderness First Responder certification. I didn't know what doors might open, but I knew that if I could pinpoint a career within the outdoor adventure industry, I would most likely need a WFR. Being a wilderness guide or something along those lines has always had its romantic appeal to the outdoorsman and explorer in me. And with that, I set off to be an NAU Lumberjack for a few weeks.

It felt like the course finished too quickly. Yes, I had received an exhaustive education in the discipline of emergency outdoor medicine. No, I didn't have a plan for what I was to do with my newly acquired credentials. My two weeks living in the motel across the street from campus ended, and I drove south to Sedona. I didn't know much about Sedona except that my dad had loved it because of its highly spiritual, new-age culture– a movement in which he immersed himself for his final eight or ten years. Sedona has traditionally been rumored among the new-agers to be geographically located in the heart of supernatural phenomena known as energy vortexes. With the same six brain cells I once used to reason that Greece was paramount to my existential journey, I also figured that Sedona might mystically hold those answers I had been seeking like magic beans.

Guess what. Sedona was boring as fuck. Beautiful? Check. Laid back? Check. Outdoor adventures? Check. The average age of your typical resident? Seventy-something– at least by the straw poll measure of my own brown peepers. After spending no more than two days there and feeling my way around for the locals' pulse, it was obvious that I had to keep moving. No adventure outfits seemed to be looking for help, and there were no more than two legit fine-dining establishments for me to apply to and float my time until peak outdoor adventure season. I called my cousin Scott and told him to clear off his couch. I was coming to surf it for a while down in L.A. I set off for Westwood, to be specific.

It didn't make a whole lot of sense. Armed with a fresh certification to work in the outdoor adventure industry, Los Angeles couldn't have been much further from my target market. But, like always, hardline reason was demoted to my deliberative backburner. Improv, once again, shuffled its way to the front. I grew up visiting Southern California almost annually, as my mom's family is mostly from there. It was mid-January, and for the first time in my 26 years, I had an opportunity to live somewhere warm and quasi-exotic during the winter months; remember, I'm Nebraskan and spent the last seven seasons blanketed by the snow of the high Rockies. Scooter had a place for me to crash, and

I had heard good things about San Diego from several people while living in Aspen.

Not since I was maybe 16 had I any suspicion whatsoever that I would ever want to live in L.A. It was an essential and idyllic destination for my youth travels, but the reality of what people must do to make life happen there had blistered its way into my cognizance, even at a younger age. Sure, the Birds of Paradise and Indian Hawthorn may ubiquitously thrive in the utopian weather. The female populace couldn't be more robust. Elevens of the conventional ten scale infiltrate the masses as though they result from an elaborate, socially curated eugenics project. The bouquet of salty ocean air and rampant air pollution mysteriously always struck a sentimental chord with me, and my unrelenting chase for creature comforts had become as imposing as ever.

But L.A. itself, as most know, is shockingly uncleanly. It redefines all dictionary definitions of litter. It's as impersonal as it is jaded. It's unfathomably expensive in the eyes of a middle-class, midwestern Homer like me. It's a universal cautionary tale of the societal juxtaposition between the "haves" and "have-nots" and the persistently growing crevasse between them. It's one of cosmically anomalous proportions, at that.

But the real kicker for someone of my natural disposition is the over-congestion of humanity issue– namely, traffic.

Patience is a virtue I've only recently begun to address in full in my early forties. Classically, I was conditioned by my impatient father to abhor traffic in all of its forms, especially that of the vehicular variety. Numbers like 405, 5, 110, and 101 have become synonymous with death by commute, a life-sucking prognosis for an unfortunate too many. Ya– no way. The plan would be to set up temporary and rent-free shop in Westwood for a week or two. From there, I would adjust the search filter to "San Diego" and seek out various jobs and places to live on Craigslist, the online Bible for scrappers like myself, in 2009.

But Craigslist has never had any upper hand over a cosmic force like serendipity.

After setting up a temporary base camp in Scott's living room, I buzzed down to San Diego one afternoon on the first of what I had imagined to be multiple recognizance missions. As fate would have it, while taking respite from the day's travails at a cafe in Mission Hills, I happened to use my momentary pause to shoot off some random texts to some college friends I hadn't consorted with for some time. I'm not, nor have I ever been, a social media person. So, knowing what any of my more remote acquaintances are up to at any given time has never been in my cards. To my utter amazement, two of the people I reached out to not only were eager to catch up with me after a few years of dissonance, but they both also happened to live in San Diego. It turned out to be the only recon mission I would need to make.

My girlfriend from the first semester at CSU, Tara, somehow financially established a life as a social worker in the greater metropolitan area, and she lived in a house in the Hillcrest neighborhood. The house had an opening for a roommate, and it was affordable. It was a large and somewhat dated unit, built in the '40s or '50s. Deb, an eccentric but friendly woman of her early seventies, owned it. She and her late husband had bought the house decades before and raised their kids there. Deb maintained her bedroom in the back and would only periodically inhabit it whenever she was in San Diego. She made Juneau, Alaska, her permanent outpost in the late '90s and kept the California house as a mainstay rental and part-time crash pad.

Even though Deb only lived in the rental 90% of the year, she militantly insisted on keeping it in its perfectly static, stylistically antiquated, and dust-covered glory, no matter the case. As her plan stood, she had less than a month to go until she was to head back to the sticks, and Deb wanted to fill a spare bedroom that she had been recently using as storage space. Jackpot!– at least in a few weeks.

I was anything but amped to share my space with an anal retentive septuagenarian, but suffering her repeated dissertations on how properly to sanitize the shower after each use or how logistically best to load a washing machine, would be relatively short-lived.

It didn't matter all that much. Tara was fantastic. She and I had maintained a healthy and respectful relationship throughout our time at CSU, and it was simply fun and comforting to be back in her presence. As one can infer from her previously noted profession, Tara was and always will be one of the most selfless and omni-loving human beings I should ever be so lucky to meet in this life. Even from age 19, when we first met, it was painfully evident that she was infinitely more well-rounded, altruistic, and emotionally mature than me. That she broke things off with me come the second semester of freshman year was a blow at the time, but in hindsight, it makes perfect sense. She was plainly out of my league by almost all measures. Even so, I loved the idea of being back around her in any capacity.

Plus, the third roommate of the house was a particularly likable thirty-something lab scientist, Raymond. He always had a smile on his face. He was pleasant to no end. He was unabashedly and aggressively a geek for all things science, and best of all, he was hardly ever around. My correspondence with Tara fatefully provided the necessary lily pad for my landing on the next chapter of my life's adventure.

My other local contact was a girl named Shannon. Shannon and I tried to date our junior year, but there wasn't much chemistry. We made much better friends. Outside of Tara, she was the only female from my college experience I would ever again interface with. Born of the down-home roots of Covington, Kentucky, she was a bastion of authenticity and the most dutiful of friends anyone could ever hope to make. Fortunately for me, she, her boyfriend, and his fledgling punk band (Local Blue) had all relocated from Crested Butte, CO, to Ocean Beach one month before my arrival. They, too, were improvising a newfound SoCal life of their own. They lived one block from the ocean and were plain old fun to be around. Much like the namesake of their music genre, they lived out a relatively "punk rock" existence– again, coming from my limited, cornfed point of view. They were non-conformist. They were genuine. They had appropriately outrageous fashion tendencies and could skateboard like the locals. They partied and socially fit in their new surroundings– something I wouldn't say I ever managed to achieve myself. They brought me under their communal wing and gave me a social refuge to be my unfiltered, non-curated self. Under their tutelage, I even learned to love Sex Pistols, NoFX, Pennywise, and Social Distortion, among other indispensable punk influences. They were not only my pals, but they were my cultural translators. I had all of the essential social necessities accounted for.

The most daunting dragon to slay took the form of sustainable employment. For two or three weeks, I would typically see my way over to the punk rock house and spend most of the day sitting with them, the lot of us looking to finance our fantasies. With my monetary resources bleeding away by the minute, I applied to every semi-respectable fine-dining server opening in the greater 40-mile radius. There were hundreds of applicants for every listing, an occurrence unlike anywhere else I had ever lived. Even chain restaurants were no shoo-in. By sheer magic, my time at Bellissima had impressed the tasting room manager at a North County winery enough that I won myself an interview. He ultimately hired me as a tasting room attendant, and I immediately took to the opportunity. The fundamental problem was that it paid $15/hr. plus tips, averaging around the $20 mark– a token wage for the fiscal realities of Southern California.

The job itself was pretty incredible. Set in what most of my patrons insisted was the best vineyard and winery in the San Pasqual Valley, the tasting room was a 10 AM-4 PM blast. I bullshitted my way into the position, professing to have a profound appreciation for everything in the world of wine. The truth was that it all tasted like dry and dusty grape drink. My only previous experience with it was memorizing the senior servers' upsells and erratically trying to regurgitate them to the diners of Bellisima, who were far more educated on the matter than me. Wine was nonsensical and overrated, but I needed a job, and the place was a constant flow of flirtatious women. Aside from the tasting room manager, I was the only guy on a staff of six or seven attendants, and I often found myself the center of sexual objectification. Both coworkers and patrons teasingly (and sometimes seriously) sexually harassed me all the time, and the 26-year-old me was an anthropomorphized "pig in shit." Rarely did my flirtations lead to any real action, but I loved the novelty nonetheless. I've never been a showstopper by any stretch, so any chance to get the hot-girl treatment in my life has always been welcome– no questions asked.

Within two days, I surprised myself and discovered that I actually not only liked wine, but I really liked it. I've never "loved" any alcohol in my life. "Really like" is the highest I can go on the substance scale, seeing as how alcohol's effects have never jibed particularly well with my physiology. I was built for cannabis and its derivatives. But at the winery, I learned that New World, Rhone-style reds are nothing to sneeze at. Syrah, Petite Sirah, Grenache, and their buddies must have been hiding from me, as Bellisima surely must've had a few lurking among their eclectic California selection. Even so, I found them when it mattered. And in very little time, I had no spiels to pedal. I only had honest reviews of distinctive blends, none of which tasted like the leathery ass sweat of my grandfather's wallet. I was to sip wine, smoke cigs on break, and flirt with bored Southern California housewives all day. Minus the pay scale, the vineyard life was not the worst chapter of my employment history.

I treasured the winery, but I had to find a supplemental income. For a minute, it looked like my impulsive decision to procure my WFR certification was of divine orchestration. Pairing my customer service résumé with my wilderness credentials scored me a part-time gig as a kayak and snorkel guide in La Jolla. For those unfamiliar with the San Diego area, La Jolla is roughly the S.D. equivalent of Aspen. It's gorgeous, happening, pricey, and there's a glut of action-adventure outfits right off of La Jolla Shores Beach. The famous sea lions of Seal Rock and the adjacent maritime caves provided the draw for the kayak tours. The leopard sharks, stingrays, and golden Garibaldis would draw the snorkelers.

I simply had to show the tourists how to explore the above without anyone drowning or me doing something wantonly stupid– or so I thought. For reasons I still don't understand, the shop's owners, Chuck and Donna, never called me in for work. It was an on-call position and seniority-based at that. I was new, but even so, there were only seven other guides on staff, and they were always hustling around. Despite their insistence that business was booming and that they thoroughly needed and appreciated me on their roster, I only ended up conducting three or four tours for the entirety of that spring and summer. It wasn't enough income to cover the investment in my wetsuit.

The only bonus of my continued affiliation with them was my ability to walk into the shop anytime and use whatever rentals were on site. I would periodically grab snorkeling gear on weekends and spend a few hours combing around the reef. The only other shop offering I ever utilized was the occasional taming of the surfboard. By "taming," I mean me trying to ride a wave for over ten feet on a ten-foot board and not killing myself in the process. This would be the childhood equivalent of successfully riding a bike with training wheels down the length of your driveway. After once riding a two-foot wave a good 50 yards to shore, I called it good. It was fun, but the learning curve was way steeper than snowboarding, and I never caught the bug enough to want to take it any further. Plus, you never hear about anyone getting eaten by prehistoric fish when riding down snowy mountains– a remote though sinister possibility that resided within my subconscious while snorkeling, as well.

It was sometime in late July or early August when, during the middle of my early afternoon shift in the tasting room, I received a phone call from one of my former Aspen roommates. I grew very close with my roommates from my second (and final) renting/living setup in Aspen. Unlike the CPA I had initially moved in with upon arrival to town, the four guys I slummed it with on the backend of that era were much more my age and demographic. We all worked service jobs, and in that socio-economic environment, it wasn't hard to find mutual brotherhood therein.

"Yo, B.J.," I answered the phone. "What's the problem? Did Vance crawl in your bed naked again?" Vance was our omni-lovable, party animal roommate. He was always happy. Vance was the most likable person in any room of any size and at any time. He was an ace with the ladies and a regular comedian with the guys. In fact, he would happily push the envelope with his comedy, sometimes stripping naked and unsolicitedly crawling into bed with B.J., the youngest and most conservative of the bunch of us. There was nothing sexual about it. He just knew how to land a perfect joke, and it never failed to get a laugh from the house.

"Vance is dead," B.J. steamrolled my cheery greeting. Not one for eloquence, he just laid it out there in three syllables. "Carter (Vance's younger brother and regular couch surfer of the house) went to wake him up this morning, and he was cold to the touch. We don't know what happened, but he was out partying with Bjorn all night, and now he's dead."

I was stunned, though by no means was this phone call made from the same dimension where my father and hero chose to end his life. I loved Vance as much as any of my friends, which is to say, an ungodly amount. That said, I was tragically fortunate in the sense that because of the magnitude of my previous trauma, I didn't require someone to prepare me by insisting I needed to sit down before receiving this message. I didn't require it to be delivered with even a pittance of bedside manner. I was devastated to hear the news, indeed. Yet, in the moment, I found myself more at an intellectual loss for how Vance could be dead rather than instantly realizing the complete annihilation of my entire emotional universe.

Nonetheless, a dear friend and peer of mine was gone, and he was found in my old bedroom and on my old mattress to make things that much more surreal. As B.J. went on to inform me, the coroner had just left the condo with Vance's body, and the autopsy wouldn't be concluded for a couple of weeks. It didn't matter. When he mentioned Bjorn, we both knew what most likely went down.

I'm fortunate to say I never had the displeasure of meeting this Bjorn character. But, after I left town, Vance started partying with a much different crowd than our core group, and this group typically revolved around a Scandinavian of a most disreputable nature. I had heard of Bjorn when I first moved to town, but remarkably, we never crossed paths. His story is that he came to town in the early '90s and made himself a laundered fortune thanks to a cocaine distribution racket disguised as a landscaping and snow removal business. As soon as he "legitimized" his ill-gotten gains, he jumped into the haute couture fashion business. I'm not going to say which brand, but he was known to be highly associated with one of the major high-end fashion retailers in town, and it just so happened to be the one where Vance worked. Whether the brand employed Bjorn or not was inconsequential. What was relevant was that whenever there was high-society deviance to be had, it frequently transpired at Bjorn's house of decadence and debauchery. The employees and management of Vance's employer were no strangers to his house on Red Mountain.

But it wasn't cocaine that was the drug primarily associated with Bjorn. Cocaine was all over Aspen, and accurate to the typecasts of the local culture since the '70s and '80s, it wasn't regarded as that big of a deal. No, Bjorn was associated mainly with heroin. From what I understand, he was no longer a black market profiteer but a more financially enabled user of its various offerings. As such, he would regularly host all-out benders for people at his luxurious compound; purportedly, anything was permitted. As was rumored, Bjorn's usual fix was injecting himself with speedballs, a mix of cocaine and heroin. His actual claim to being a piece of shit was that he got several other people acquainted with and ultimately consumed by the aforementioned deadly concoction.

We never did get a final answer on how Vance died. Carter had taken over as the legal representation for Vance's affairs, and when he got the report, he wouldn't tell anyone the results. Not only that but once Vance's ashes were disbursed among his family and friends, Carter quit talking to all of us. He packed up his car, drove back home to Biloxi, changed his phone number, and has seemingly never spoken with anyone from his Aspen experience ever again. I can't blame him. The party scene in that town stole his big brother and best friend from him. I hope he forever remembers me as someone who wholesomely loved him and Vance. It wasn't the anguish of a missing father, but I was markedly sad to have lost those two as adoptive brothers of my own choosing.

By early fall, the practical reality of what I had to do to cover my monthly nut in Southern California became transparently unachievable. I was commuting 45 minutes each way to and from Escondido in North County, and every month, I was coming in upside down on my finances. Tara had gotten a job offer in Denver and began packing up for her imminent move back home. Ironically, the punk rock house also could never establish a sound enough collective base of income, so they, too, not only had to relocate but would be breaking up as a band and moving off on their separate ways. I was losing whatever facets of familiar comforts I had discovered, and my internal Bat Signal to skip town and start my existence over took to the sky. I had to break inertia once again.

As the old cliche goes, "It's not *what* but rather *who* you know." I knew an old college buddy who was reportedly killing it as a resort concierge in South Lake Tahoe, and he, much like Holly in Aspen, knew all of the big players in the local service industry. With the push of "send" on Mikey's contact in my cell phone, the odyssey would continue. Just like that, my Ford Escape was again packed to the brim, and north I steered her on I-15.

California Gleaning: Part 2

It was late September, and the massive influx of seasonal service workers had yet to flood the job market. As Mikey pointed out, between the time I decided I was on my way to try on Sierra Life and the time I got to town, the seas parted, and a minor miracle materialized for me from nowhere. In his usual dealings with local restaurants, the owner of one of South Lake's two most well-reputed restaurants lamented that one of his longtime employees had to make an emergency, long-term relocation back to the Bay Area. His restaurant only employed three servers at any given time, as it was a tiny Italian chalet retrofitted from an old 400-square-foot cabin. The dining room wasn't even half that size, so he kept his payroll at minimal employees. With such physical limitations to the amount of patrons they could serve on any given night, a large percentage of his revenue was predicated on wine sales. There was no bar, but the food was immaculate (Zagat-rated), and the wine wasn't cheap. Plus, the bottles seemed to sell themselves effortlessly.

On my second day in town– almost a Groundhog Day-like repeat of my first foray into Aspen– Mikey walked me into Bolzano, and out I walked with a job. It was the best fine-dining service job in North America, and I'll happily die on that hill of a statement. The owner, Lance, was the kindest of restaurateurs I've ever met, bar none. He was physically reminiscent of Rick Morannis but somehow even more friendly, disarming, and of a habitual benevolence that would give any financial advisor chills to the core. He was apparently from Louisiana, but you would never know it with his perfect absence of any southern accent. Lance was also a second-level sommelier and an extremely engaging one at that. He routinely opened bottles we had on the menu listed between $100-$500+, simply so he could enjoy and discuss them with his well-tenured staff and treasured clientele.

The food was inscrutably the tastiest and most consistently executed fare I was ever so lucky to serve. I legitimately don't recall ever having to return even one dish to the chef to be remade. And, unlike many other kitchen personalities I had encountered over the years, this kitchen staff was mesmerizingly happy and playful. Run by a naturalized Mexican immigrant and self-trained chef, Cortez was a man truly unlike most kitchen leaders. In addition to being unflappably joyous, he always seemed to be whistling, singing ludicrous lyrics to fictitiously improvised songs, or laughing with his crew. His team was a few of his cousins and another guy from their home village. The sous chef, Pelon, was a hysterical character, down for a good joke 100% of the time. His favorite schtick was to loudly proclaim that Ubaldo— the sweet, quiet, exceedingly bashful, and youngest of the cousins in the kitchen— wanted to be my boyfriend, but he was too shy to ask me out. Ubaldo would blush one thousand times out of a thousand, and all of us would die laughing. I loved playing the part of Ubaldo's hypothetical novio, frequently winking and making kissy faces to him. Anything for the kitchen crew— that's the first cardinal rule of serving.

One summer night, as I was cleaning off a table on the outdoor patio, I thought I saw my grandfather's ghost for a fleeting second. After overhearing Lance check in two elderly patrons under the reservation of "Melvin," I happened to look up and see my long lost Great Uncle Melvin (and his doll of a wife, Joan) standing in the doorway, resembling a spitting image of his long-deceased older brother, Harold.

"Melvin Perelman?" I stammered, still in visceral disbelief, mentally processing the sheer unbelievability of the situation. He and Joan looked at me with almost as dumbfounded expressions splayed across their faces.

"Yes," he impulsively replied. "How did you know that?" It was readily apparent to all of us that he had only booked with his first name.

"You're my uncle," I shot back with no soft opening. "Your brother was my Grandpa Harold. I'm Shelly's youngest, Zachary."

With that, a new bridge of insight into my father's family and legacy was gifted to me by this astronomically improbable occurrence. After a solid 10 to 15 minutes of catching up on 20 years of history, we decided it would behoove all of us for me to join them for dinner at their lakehouse the next night. A long time before I ever remotely thought I'd live in California, I vaguely recall having heard Uncle Mel had a place up in Tahoe. It wouldn't dawn on me in a thousand lifetimes that he might ever cross my path. Of the three brothers, he was financially the most successful after having served a long career as C.E.O. and Chairman of the Board of one of the major American pharmaceutical manufacturers. My grandpa and his younger brother, Bob, did well for themselves, but Mel made it big.

The invaluable thing I learned about my Great Uncle Melvin was that he was not only financially successful but also grounded and charming. Having long established his primary existence in Indianapolis, he took to the horse racing culture and was a horse breeder for some time, if I recall correctly. Also, he was once considered one of the most prominent private collectors of Native American artifacts in the country. Say what you will about cultural appropriation, but he genuinely exuded a respect and fondness for Native culture from what I could tell– a trait common to us both. He was fascinating. He was unconventional. He was kind. The short rendezvous I was afforded with the last remaining Perelman of that generation was an unexpected treat. He reminded me that my father's side of the family was elementally comprised of good people. For what they collectively lacked in emotional wherewithal, they made up for with straightforward, no-nonsense decency. I'll forever cherish this blurb of a revelatory experience with my dear old Uncle Mel (and Joan).

Even though I lived no more than three blocks from the California base of Heavenly, and the region is famously known for its bountiful snowfalls for wintertime sports, the crown jewel season was irrefutably summer. As much as I did appreciate the local winter offerings, the draw of the lake was far more alluring and valuable to me than anything associated with my seasonal ski pass. In the summer, the roads were easy peasy, so circling the lake and looking for random adventures on either side presented no shortage of possibilities. More often than not, I'd find myself with Jenna (my girlfriend at the time) on the northeast Nevada side of the lake, sunbathing on massive boulders on the shoreline. You simply had to park on the shoulder and hike down the embankment a few yards, and there was site after site of semi-private coves to choose from. And the clarity of the lake was second to none. Even for a germophobe weiner like me, periodically wading around that lake never felt like recreating in someone else's pissy bathwater.

However, after seven seasons of scouring Colorado's best slopes and small-town cultures– with much drier and more pleasurable snowfalls to play in– I was highly unimpressed with South Lake's winters compared to anything I had previously experienced. The Sierras hold nothing over the Rockies in these regards. And it would be integral to mention that South Lake's biggest problem is that it isn't a ski town; it's a casino town. Yes, it hosts Heavenly and sits relatively adjacent to Kirkwood, Northstar, Sierra, and other worthwhile ski destinations. A vast portion of the lake's encircling communities have their livelihoods depend on the ski industry. Even so, South Lake itself felt transient and overly commercialized. Every weekend, regardless of season, it would draw in some serious specimens from Sacramento and the greater Bay Area, and whatever was "happening" was typically transpiring in one of its handful of third-rate casinos. If Reno wishes it was Vegas– and it does– then South Lake wishes it was Reno– facts.

Additionally, there is no semblance of a downtown or civic center of any sort. The closest thing would be the gondola plaza at Heavenly, which, as far as I can tell, doesn't exactly constitute municipal infrastructure or organic cultural history. Between that base village of overpriced tourist traps on the far east side of town and the entire length of Highway 50 spanning to the far west of city limits, the town's narrative appeared as though everybody simply quit trying sometime circa the mid-'70s. Things may have changed as of the writing of this memoir, but in the early 2010s, the facade of that entire stretch of town was tired to a degree of narcolepsy. Shleppy motels, hokey souvenir shops, and chain restaurant after chain restaurant comprised the soul of Tahoe Boulevard; Denny's was a staple.

After three years of thoroughly enjoying the fruits of Aspen– a culturally superlative existence over South Lake– I knew deep down that I wouldn't ever be able to sit still and start building a life where I found myself. This familiar brand of restlessness felt familiar, but at least this time, I was learning how to channel it properly to some degree. In South Lake, I discovered the art and gift of running. Predominantly one of my least favorite pastimes, cardio, suddenly and out of a black hole of nothingness overtook my downtime fixations. It started with a mile here or two there. In a few short months, my anxiety and resultant need for cathartic release would eventually see me looping through town on six-, seven-, or eight-mile jaunts. It was a perfect elixir until it wasn't.

By April of 2011, the writing was etched upon a stone wall– gas up my steed, pack her to the brim, and toggle my G.P.S. This time, there was no indeterminate destination for me to load in my search bar. Punching "Denver" into my Google Maps that day was perhaps the easiest and most comforting single word I'd ever submitted to the Google platform. It had been over two years since I left, but there was no longer sense in denying it. Colorado was my home, and life in the diaspora had progressively grown more disenchanting and wearisome. It was time to go home before I, too, became a narcoleptic fixture of South Lake.

Coloradhome

Once again, much like post-Europe, I missed Colorado dearly, and as soon as I decided that California was a failed endeavor from bottom to top, my wick was lit. I had recently received a small inheritance from my father's minimal estate, so heedlessly relinquishing the lucrative life of Bolzano and starting all over was suddenly a financially viable option. On my voyage, I ate nothing. I smoked a whole pack of Spirits and guzzled Red Bulls. Forever captive to the disruption of my circadian rhythms, I had no other choice. I wasn't hungry, and sleep– as physiologically indispensable as it may be– was simply time wasted away from my element.

I made the 16-hour drive home in 18, stopping only four times– thrice to piss and gas up and once to nod off for a power nap on the shoulder of the road. When I finally pulled into town, I wasn't even remotely tired. The adrenaline of moving to Denver, paired with my natural slap-happy response to overnight sleep deprivation, had me mysteriously crisp and focused. I set out for my sister's house, where I could park my car and buy myself a moment to use her basement as my planning space. It would serve as much for two weeks until I found myself a decent one-bedroom apartment in Uptown. The building was of the typical early to mid-20th-century variety for that part of Denver. The unit looked like it hadn't been renovated in several decades, but it was clean, affordable, and 100% just for me.

It wasn't until that budget spot off of 16th and Washington that I had ever had the opportunity to live entirely independently. From freshman year at CSU until the end of my time in Tahoe, I had always had roommates, typically guys. It wasn't until I was afforded this unparalleled amenity that I learned how utterly essential it was for someone of my specific cut. Whether it is the product of my being a distant third in my family's generational order and having my siblings leave me as a virtual only-child as they went off to college, or whether

I've always been a loner at heart, but maintaining an exclusive temple of personal space quickly became a lifestyle that suited my every need. No more dirty dishes in the sink or other people's intrusive girlfriends instructing me what I should be doing to find a girlfriend of my own. Nope. No longer my problems.

My sweltering, non-air-conditioned, thinly-walled rental was a palace. It was within walking distance to everything fun in the heart of Denver, and there was a dispensary not 30 yards away from my building's back alley dumpster. A portable A/C and some of my neighbor's medicinal offerings would serve perfectly as suitable remedies for my unit's deficiencies. The parking situation was a nightly fiasco, but memorizing the fire lanes and street-by-street sweeping schedule was simply part of the production.

In short order, I would become a regular at the neighbor's dope shop and land myself a solid prospect of a serving job down by the Convention Center, some place called Section 37. After leaving Tahoe, I swore to myself that I would explore any feasible option for work before returning to the fine dining industry. There was no way I could find anything as cushy and wholesomely rewarding as working at Bolzano. When you figured California minimum wage into the hourly tips, it was insanely livable, especially when you figured for the lovability of the kitchen crew and Lance. Additionally, I was in my late twenties, and the fact that I had a college degree going perfectly unutilized began to bear a bristly reality. It's not like I ever had an inkling what one was to do with a Liberal Arts education, but I never figured that acting out the role of waiting tables would lead to such pesky "golden handcuffs."

Serving more than paid my modest bills. It afforded me free meals cooked by bona fide professionals. It allowed me the ability to sleep in every day– my body's natural heroin addiction since I was a young boy. I met countless women weekly. After walking to and from work and serving tables all night, I'd typically get in a good 15,000-20,000 steps per working day. When you combine that with the fact that my growing existential anxiety had me running 40-60 miles per week, I finally entered a domain I had always fantasized about– I was a hot body. My dad bod of terminal childhood memory was all of a sudden a thing of the past.

At one point, when I was both dieting and running laps around Denver, I got myself down to 158 lbs. of lean muscle mass. I had definition. I had the faint beginnings of a six-pack. I looked great naked– finally! I was habitually getting laid like it was college spring break in Cancun. And....I was at the absolute breaking point, feeling that I had failed my most authentic self. The dieting, the running, the partying, the promiscuity– all of it– were other distractions, albeit ones of physically healthy enterprise. Not only is there nothing wrong with the previously listed outlets of human activity, but those are all indispensably beneficial practices when done in moderation and not used excessively as diversionary tactics. I preferred the diversions.

My health-centric excesses were so indulged that I figured, for posterity's sake, I'd harvest their fruits and run a marathon or two. And that's what I did. After hustling around serving tables all night, the restlessness I was experiencing on a nightly basis forced me out of my apartment and onto the streets of Denver for up to three hours a jaunt. Before I knew it, I was running 20+ miles after any given shift and often until 4 AM. It only made sense to justify this behavior with a good old-fashioned race. It was me against me. Winner takes nothing.

In 2012, I completed the Rock 'n Roll Marathon Denver in 3:49:54. I followed that up in 2013 with a time of 3:50:44. I was in peak physical condition and a teeming stew of emotional despair. For how accomplished I felt with my bodily transformation, I felt doubly disappointed with the trajectory of my professional orbit. Even though I've always been raised to believe that pursuits of such a corporeal nature will inevitably prove vapid, I had to discover this reality on my own merits for its teachings to be effectively taught. My cultivated physique held no jurisdiction in the forum of my innermost self. Plus, plantar fasciitis is a real phenomenon, and after two years and thousands of miles of ground covered, my existential avoidance left me barely able to walk.

The cosmos gifted me a Godsend, which came in the form of nepotism. In May of 2013, I was beyond wit's end with my time at Section 37, and I was offered a chance to make a massive career jump by my second cousin, Chaz. He was the CEO and partial owner of a legitimate, vertically integrated cannabis enterprise, Skyward Farms, and he needed a trustworthy individual to replace one of his full-time growers. Not only was prior experience in cultivation not necessary, but the prevailing managerial strategy within the cannabis production industry has conventionally been to find good workers with zero experience so you can train them your way and not have to police and rehab their preexisting bad habits. I was a perfect fit for the job. I knew how to hustle and sweat at work. I had a résumé chock full of glowing contacts. I was dying to switch careers, and the subject matter of the enterprise could not have been more up my alley of recreational preoccupations. And I was "good people." In a sector of the economy primarily run at the time by yesteryear's black-market felons, that was by far my finest attribute.

So it was settled. I would forever cast my server's apron to the annals of history and try my hand as a grunt in the garden. The transition was as literally and figuratively as intoxicating as my high-school self could have dreamed up in my wildest imaginings. Not only did I not have to interface with the hangry antics of the general public, but I also got to spend my days watering plants and blasting music on a loudspeaker, all the while sporting basketball shorts and flip-flops. At first, that was precisely my mindset. Then, the novelty naturally wore off within a few short weeks, and work became work.

And growing dope is not nearly as leisurely and carefree as most would like to assume. In fact, it is a ton of back-breaking labor that resides well within the realm of stone-cold monotony. Everything is part of a process, and every process is to be replicated day after day, week after week, or cycle after cycle. The cyclical nature of the repeated horticultural processes is an overarching reality that a person either grows to love or learns to despise. Unlike serving, each day had its codified routines, the predictability of which was infinitely more like clockwork. Sure, it was priceless to understand better what my working days might entail versus the sheer unknown of what any given night at the restaurant might present. In cultivation, once the Standard Operating Procedures are established, the indoor environment is stabilized, your genetic library of cannabis strains is set, and you have a team of savvy workers, the rest typically goes according to the anticipated plan. Since cannabis flowering cycles generally run eight weeks, every last facet of the operation was predicated on an 8-week cycle of rinse and repeat. We had eight flowering rooms, and they were all perfectly staggered in age one week apart from the next. This would make it so that every week, we would clone, prune, harvest, transplant, mix soil, supervise temp-worker trimmers, spray pesticides (twice per week), etc. The only variable that changed was which service(s) we performed in what room, based on how far along each room was in its respective 8-week cycle.

It was a very straightforward proposition. As a facility under 5,000 square feet, it would initially require only three employees to keep our heads above water. Clay Bowers was the Director of Cultivation, and under him, the operation was run by a staff of three. Above me was the lead-grower, Darren. He was my direct-report supervisor and would ultimately teach me 90% of everything I know about the best practices of green-thumb gardening. Originally a black market grower from Florida, he and Clay discovered each other a few years before my arrival, and the two of them developed a functional, though continuously developing, design for a legitimate cannabis operation.

Darren worked hand-in-hand with Kerry, the gal who would not just help Darren and me when we needed the hands during major planting/harvesting operations, but she also was in charge of compliance, pre-planning, office management, and correspondence with our retail locations. Between Kerry, Darren, and myself, we were tasked with ensuring the unending circuit of eight weeks for this or eight weeks for that persisted in perfect perpetuity.

Let's say that everything I just logistically mapped out was much more of an "on-paper" proposition than a static reality of the real world. In all actuality, the operation was perfectly imperfect. The space in which we operated was a basic office building with its superficial amenities stripped away, leaving behind not much more than a series of 11 separate growing rooms (eight for flowering plants and three for vegetative plants). To say that during those pioneering years of the industry (around 2009), ownership didn't know what they didn't know about commercial cannabis production would be an obscene understatement. Based on how the laws were initially written for the Colorado Medical Cannabis industry, no entity was allowed to build new production facilities from the ground up. It was the state's attempt to help gentrify numerous failing industrial neighborhoods within greater Denver. The policy would cause entrepreneurs like the owners of Skyward to acquire old and often ramshackle properties in these neighborhoods and force them to invest heavily in substandard infrastructures. Commercial rents, previously going for a few hundred bucks a month, suddenly skyrocketed to thousands upon thousands of dollars monthly. More often than not, like in the case of Skyward, this policy created undue financial challenges and categorically set up the entire industry for considerable operational issues for many years to come.

Our facility was the quintessential case in point of the long-term shortsightedness of Colorado lawmakers in how they initially designed the laws governing production within such a nascent industry. In short, we were legally forced to farm in a building designed for anything but accommodating 6,000 living, breathing, respiring organisms of a botanical nature. There wasn't a floor drain in any of the 11 rooms. Because of the processes involved in the flowering of cannabis, the room doors had to remain shut for the vast majority of every day. This would preserve the strict regimen of 12 hours of light and 12 hours of perfect darkness for the plants and maintain the proper ratio of heat and moisture in any given room. The inherent problem with this? The walls were standard dry-wall, basic porous tiling comprised the ceilings, and the HVAC system for each room was erratic at best.

When restricted to the parameters I previously listed, maintaining the optimal environment for thriving cannabis comes directly at odds with mold mitigation. In less than a year or so, every room in the joint had black mold accruing behind every wall. By the end of the four or five years in that particular operation, more locations than not on any section of drywall could be effortlessly pushed inward due to rampant mold rot.

As gross as it was, the first year or two of this phenomenon was brushed off more as a cosmetic than a practical issue. The plants were regularly producing, and the quality was as high as any of our competitors. As a side note, over the years of my being a part of that enterprise, our outfit took home innumerable awards and distinctions based on the quality of the product we routinely submitted to *High Times Cannabis Cup*, *Rooster Cup*, or *Hemp Connoisseur Magazine* competitions– The Big Three, back then. Clay and Darren knew how to mass-produce flower of the highest quality. That was never the issue. Our biggest problem– as well as that of virtually all of our competition– became not just to produce the highest quality dope in the most considerable quantities possible but to have our final product routinely pass the newly instituted microbial testing mandate enacted by the state– years after the gentrification mandate.

Simply put, we were all indoor farmers producing regulated products in buildings that weren't designed to do anything of the sort– at least not per best practices. Before we knew it, we, and many of our competitors, were stuck with hundreds of pounds of products we couldn't sell because they were microbially contaminated well beyond the threshold of what's considered acceptable by production standards. Some of the failed products could be remediated into concentrates or edibles but for mere pennies on the dollar of what we'd otherwise generate if left as regular flower. Just like that, the industry producers found themselves in quite the quagmire of paying exorbitant rents to slumlords, all so that come harvest time, more of their final product than not was determined to be unfit for human consumption. Add to this, around the same time, Colorado tamped down exceptionally hard on the use of chemical pesticides, so many of the unpronounceable names of the active ingredients we could once use to battle microbes successfully were all of a sudden ruled off limits for all legal purposes. Instead of spraying a room once every few weeks with a pesticide that actually worked, we were forced to quadruple our frequency of delivery but with hippie-dippie organics like citric acid, peppermint oil, neem, diatomaceous earth, and a whole bunch of other snake oil that hardly accomplishes it's intended purpose on any sort of an industrial scale.

Ultimately, our biggest challenge wasn't nourishing and maintaining plant health as much as it was "gaming" our highly imperfect building to keep meeting production quotas without sacrificing profits to failed microbial testing. I liken it to a real-world game of *Mousetrap*. For those unfamiliar with the 1980s board game, *Mousetrap*, instead of a traditional board game, is more of a series of makeshift contraptions that successfully physically stimulate one another, much like the falling of dominoes. It was more of a gimmicky toy than a game of competition. Its premise is something like starting by rolling a ball, which falls into a basket, which moves a lever, which pushes a button, which drops a weight, etc. The end goal is to get the last of the chain reactions to drop a laundry-basket-looking cage down a pole and trap the immobile, plastic mouse in its place.

Our version of *Mousetrap* had exponentially more variables. Still, it was essentially the same– figure out the natural environmental tendencies of each highly unique growing space and continuously maintain eight weeks' worth of chain reactions, hoping that by the end of any given cycle, the final product was ample, high-quality, and clean. But as I noted, each room– for whatever mysterious reason of the cosmos– ran slightly differently from each other. Despite everyone's best attempt at initially setting up each room with as much uniformity as the next, the sheer fact is that each room was its own beast.

Rooms on the south side of the building would naturally warm up faster than those on the north side. Depending on the varying size of each room, one might require more dehumidification than the next. Or, due to variances in sizing, certain rooms might require more of this or less of that. Bigger room? More plants. More plants equal more feed water. More feed water equals more runoff. More runoff equals higher humidity. Higher humidity equals more dehumidifier action. More dehumidifier action equals more room heat. More room heat equals more air-conditioning. More air conditioning equals more power load on the building. More power load on the building equals blackouts. Blackouts equal mass chaos and, ultimately, large-scale failure. It was a balancing act of the most precarious sort, and any slight disturbance of the constants set in place would irretrievably throw the whole ecosystem out of whack.

And then there were the tendencies of the strains themselves. We always had at least two dozen distinct strains in our library, each with its own nitpicky environmental preferences to varying degrees. Some liked growing in this room– others, not so much. Some strains preferred to grow directly under the grow lights, whereas others may utterly abhor such direct intensity. Some were big hitters in their ability to generate a lot of weight per plant, but their sex appeal on the retail shelf was no longer en vogue. Or one strain might produce championship-level quality buds in terms of smell, smoke, and flavor, but the living organisms themselves would lack the genetic predisposition to fight off powdery mildew and botrytis (bud rot) successfully– ultimately rendering them habitual losers come time for microbial testing. All factors were to be considered every time we planted a room, and there was no perfect algorithm for success.

Sure, botany is a science. But successfully running a commercial cannabis production in the early days was far more of an art. And it was an art that would prove to be considerably more challenging to comprehensively understand than I ever would have guessed from the outset.

Much like most worthwhile endeavors, the art of cannabis cultivation is grounded in the virtue of patience, universally one of my less-boastworthy attributes. Everything is a process. Time to break up soil and fill up dirtbags? Set up a repeatable process in the dirt room, and three or four sweaty hours later, we'd have a few hundred bags awaiting tomorrow's transplant. Need clones for room six? Spend a few hours chopping, chopping, chopping away at the mother stock in veg room two. It was laborious in every sense of the term, and once the invigorating rush of growing a universally oppressed and federally prohibited substance wore off, it actually became work. Most enthusiasts, like myself, who professionally enter the domain of their favorite vice, often find that whatever magical mystery there once was surrounding the substance of their reverence quickly fades into the realities of "how the sausage is made."

By week two, I was already lamenting that my 30-year-old body was no longer my 20-year-old body. Whereas once upon a time, the biggest pain in the ass of my working day came in the form of the occasionally pissy spa patron, I now had actual, literal pains in my ass, classified technically as sciatica. Make no mistake about it. Growing weed is farming, and farming can be purely brutal on the human body. Lift. Set. Stand. Sit. Crouch. Crawl. Twist. Yank. Water. Cut. Repeat. Repeat. Repeat. Repeat. My general lack of patience and presence within the eternal moment made the tedium of repetition my alpha complaint. I wasn't sure exactly what I had thought being a grower was like, but I hadn't imagined it would all quickly fall into the jurisdiction of being excruciatingly repetitive.

After a few months at it, I was struggling, frankly. I found it difficult for several reasons. I didn't love the grind of daily labor. Most of it felt like bitchwork at the time. It didn't pay particularly well. Plus, due to the combination of cultivation's inherent complexity and my propensity for impatience, I quickly frustrated myself to the point of unlikability among my two coworkers. It got to a point where Chaz even came over one day from the corporate office to pull me aside and tell me how much my attitude sucked. I was on the precipice of blowing my newfound career opportunity, and I had to step up my game massively. So what did I do? I stepped up my game massively.

I couldn't tell you what it says about me or the general human psyche, but in the past, whenever I've been called out for being an embarrassing version of myself, I've miraculously found this ability to rebound and rebound big time. From that moment of getting dressed down in the parking lot by Chaz and onward, I adopted an entirely different personality. Instead of being slow to execute my daily duties, I became assertive about seeking them out and how to do them in better, more innovative ways. Rather than wasting time bitching to Kerry about the lack of materials or to Darren about the imperfect structure of the irrigation lines, I challenged myself to shut my mouth and attempt mastery of our manifestly inconquerable mishmash of a production facility.

With my righting of the ship, I quickly reestablished respect among my few working associates. Clay, Kerry, and Darren were happy to start over with the new me, and I definitively seized this opportunity. There was no way I was going back to the customer service industry. Once I got the hang of our daily dance with the facility's countless nuances, making art of the procedures became quite enjoyable. For someone of my neurotic disposition– constantly yearning for order and uniformity in this disorderly world– learning how to feng shui a room full of free-standing mother plants or make a seamless hedge of rows upon rows of flowers, my daily duties transformed into rituals of wholehearted joy. Work actually became fun. For the first time in my life, "paying the man" felt like anything but.

That didn't even account for the avant-garde social experiment of our daily work breaks. The breaks took the form of what is conventionally referred to in the cannabis industry as "safety meetings," which legally had to transpire off-property and down the street along the South Platte River. We couldn't exactly just smoke the product straight out of the facility, but we all got raging discounts at our retail store and never had a shortage of variety from which to choose. But it wasn't sampling the product that made breaks at all noteworthy. The juicy part was that 80-90% of the time we would do as much, there would be loitering the regular band of miscreants we dubbed "The River People." The River People had a staple crew of four: Father Time, Nickle Tits, Skeezer, and Jug Jug. Of course, those most likely weren't their names, but based on their outward appearances and behavior, we didn't exactly take the time to initiate dignified introductions. Those names would suffice. They didn't really care to know us any more than we cared to know them. For years, we would simply view each other from a few yards apart, each group embracing the other, much like specimens studying specimens in an unregulated urban zoo.

So, we made up backstories to make sense of the River People's daily reenactment of the *Jerry Springer Show*. Father Time seemed to be the patriarch of the group. Much like you might assume by his name, he looked ancient and had a flowing white beard. In all reality, he was probably about 60, but the whole group was ostensibly on drugs– not the kind we grew– and it looked as though he put some extra miles on his ticker from the lifestyle. He drove an old blue Ford Ranger, which permanently sported a bed overflowing with junk to be scrapped. His truck was adorned with black flames sloppily sprayed on the grill with what looked to be Flex Seal sealant. It was the work of NIckle Tits. Nickles was Father Time's old lady, it seemed. She was obviously younger than him, though relatively, she hadn't aged much better. She was the most unabashed of the bunch and had no problem openly smoking from pipes that weren't designed for consuming organics. Also, she liked getting picked up and dropped off by random gentlemen multiple times daily. Father Time didn't even seem to care or even notice, for that matter. Nickel Tits ran the show. She was the madame of the mayhem.

Skeezer and Jug Jug were always in tandem, and they always had more bikes on them than the two of them could collectively pedal. Some days, they had four. Somedays, they had ten. There was always at least one bike flipped upside down with a missing wheel and a chain to be fixed. The two looked to be younger guys, maybe in their early twenties, but they appeared to operate with a savvy of world-wary street hustlers. Flipping stolen bikes might have been their day job, but we grew to believe that they might have been deep-cover Illuminati or trained assassins by night. We might have smoked entirely too much pot.

By all measures, the life of growing grass had perks unlike any other.

In roughly two years, Darren trained me to a point where I could replace him when he moved out to Las Vegas to start another cannabis company with Clay and some other investors independent of Skyward. In two short years, I, by and large, knew how the sausage was made. Whether it was when to water or how to water, what to prune and when to prune it, what to clone and how to clone it, what to look for and what to do about it, or whatever the situation, as long as Kerry and Clay remained the bedrock of the operation, I was delighted to take on more responsibility and more ownership of our communal triumphs and failures.

By the time Darren left for Vegas around 2015, I was firmly entrenched as an integral cog in the machine of Skyward's back-of-the-house operation. When I got promoted, not only was I put in the position to delegate to my replacement, Charlie, but we even brought on one more grower, David, as well as a Post-Harvest Manager, Jessica. Kerry, Jessica, Charlie, David, and I– we became the heart and soul of everything that made that company what it was. We grew Clay's dope, and Clay's dope was hands down some of the best in the land.

Ya, for a few years there, we lived in the "good ol' days," and I'm happy to say that we knew it and reveled in it as such. For all of the cancer we didn't cure and all of the planet's hungry mouths we didn't feed, we loved what we were doing. It was fun. It was informal. It paid the bills. And getting high was a prerequisite for success. All those years defying Nancy Regan's "Just Say No" campaign incidentally paid its due. To my sheer and utter delight, my professional redemption arc had been well underway. Turns out, I'd been pursuing a mastery of the cannabis arts since those early days when I waved "bye-bye" to the world of team sports and purely intellectual pursuits. I found my happy place, and my continued professional performance was crucial to its sustained existence. For a while there, things sustained. Things were better than satisfactory. The industry was (and still very much is) unpredictable, oversaturated, cutthroat, and volatile, but we were making it and basking in the uniqueness of it all. Those early years at Skyward were unequivocally some of the best of my life.

Cat's In The Courtyard

If you had surveyed me on the very first day of October 2015 and asked me if I was wholly happy, I would not have been able to look you directly in the eye and answer affirmatively. I loved work and what had become my daily grind. The more I leaned into my new identity as a cannabis grower– and a damn solid one at that– the more withdrawn I felt myself becoming from my friends, family, and the world in its entirety. I was fatigued and in so many ways. Online dating had grown tiresome and a part-time job in and of itself. I had no tiffs with any of my loved ones, yet I never felt remotely compelled to reach out to anyone in moments of downtime. I'd get up and go to work. Hustle and shake at blue-collar tasks all day. Hit the dispensary and whatever form of ethnic takeout on my way home. Then, I'd hang it up for the evening before a glowing television and with all my necessary numbing agents.

I hadn't consciously realized it, but my increasing isolation was also elevating my natural disposition of being overly moody and exceedingly directed by irrational anger. People either got it or they didn't. To me, you were essentially incredible or a schmuck, and the line between the two could jump course on you like a flash-flooded river. If you knew how to mind the fast lane of traffic, expediently check yourself out at the grocery store, or give me the right-of-way and head nod when I jogged across your motorist path, you were a rockstar. If you weren't firing on all cylinders in this sphere of life or the other, and your lack of proficiency was holding up my show, I was positively nonplussed, to say the least. More to the point, if you didn't illicit a tantalizing feeling of joy from me, I really didn't care to engage you in any fashion. It was simply more leisurely, simply more comfortable, to retreat to my cycle of sleep, wake, work, numb, repeat.

And then, naturally, the first day of October rolled into the second, as the universal order of things would dictate. It was just after lunch at the facility, and I was sitting in one of the veg rooms transplanting mother plants from 2-gallon pots to 5-gallon pots when Charlie barged in and said, "Dude, you've got to come out to the courtyard and check this out."

"Alright, man. I'll be there in a second. I'm just gonna transplant these last few," I replied before being forcefully overruled by my subordinate.

"Trust me. You want to see what we just found," he continued. That was enough to spark my interest.

Immediately upon opening the door to the courtyard in the opening walkway to the facility, I looked out to see what turned out to be a 3.3lb., 8-week-old, pure black, domestic short-hair kitten, climbing the biggest tree in the yard. We had heard from the overnight security guard that a feral kitty had been making the rounds at night and that he thought the cat was living on the roof of our facility. I hadn't thought much about it until he revealed himself to us on this very day. We all adored him at first sight (except for Dave, who didn't love much of anything except living out his role as the "Angry Hippie" of the Denver cannabis production scene).

The cat spent the rest of the afternoon shadowing us around the facility, freely wandering about our "professional" place of regulated production as we finished the day's tasks. By day's end, the inevitable conundrum presented itself. What would we do with this kitten, which was clearly stray and famished? Kerry and Jessica each had their own cats, and they insisted neither creature was taking applications for feline siblings. Charlie couldn't take him because he's allergic to basically everything except water and white bread. Obviously, Dave was a non-starter. That left me or the pound as the only two humane options. I didn't even think twice. We clocked out, and I took myself home a cat.

So here's the thing. I was conditioned never even to like cats. At a very young age, my older brother essentially taught me that it was effeminate and weak to like cats. Dogs were for boys, and cats were for girls. It was the '80s so that tracked with common logic. It was a simple enough script to play along with until it wasn't. The truth is that I've forever had this Ace Ventura-like kinship with almost all animals, and I have always secretly maintained a crush on the species. It wasn't until that afternoon in the courtyard of Skyward that I realized how grossly incorrect my indoctrination against the species was. I named him Butters and instantaneously knew he was the beginning of a brand new chapter in what had grown to become my stagnated existence.

After pulling away from work, I went straight to the grocery store, scored some kibble, and watched him feast in the front seat of my car with an appetite more voracious than that of an animal four times his size. With that, he was sold on me. The two of us were starving– he for a meal, me for some meaning. Suddenly, I was no longer just some dude who was killing it at his job, but I was a Cat Dad, and that animal depended on me. It wouldn't be until some time later that I realized it, but having something so lovable that relied solely upon me for its sustenance, comfort, and joy flipped a switch in me from apathy to empathy. This adorable little critter needed me, and that dependence awoke within me the long-buried virtue of compassion. I could deny my love no longer. It was easy not to love the women I slept with. It was easy not to love my fellow man or perfect stranger. It would be a logical fallacy of all scholastic measures not to love this quirky, spirited cartoon of a character.

When Butters was a kitten, he was a most agreeable cat, happily accompanying me in the car, running errands, or visiting my friends' houses. He was the prototypical "cool cat." People loved him, and for a while, he enjoyed people as well. That was a phase that didn't last particularly long. When he outgrew his little kitty body, he also outgrew his general amenability to humans who weren't me. By one year old, he had built himself a bit of a reputation as an irritable asshole, much like that of his doting father. Ironically, the more Butters closed himself off to the love of other humans and focused it solely on me, the more I learned to reciprocate and reawaken a sensitivity I had banished to dormancy long ago. His exclusive affection for me not only won me over on a one-to-one basis but also won my reverence for the species as a whole.

I *love* dogs. I utterly and unabashedly *love* dogs. I grew up with dogs. I grew up around dogs. Everyone had them, and they are all lovable to varying degrees– minus a few lap dogs. That said, I'm now a cat person because of Butters and his unnegotiable stubbornness of character. Unlike dogs, cats really don't give a shit what you think or what your agenda might happen to be. Although I know there are exceptions to the generalization– as there always are– these creatures steeped in the art of nonconformity have so much unwavering gumption to be themselves that they should be the official mascot of the inclusivity movement. Mark that as my official nomination.

Butters won me over with his insistence on annoyance. He loved waking me at all hours. He murdered all of my house plants. His favorite hobby was chewing through my phone chargers. He loved knocking whole packages of eggs off the counter for no good reason. He played with his claws fully extended, and of course, he never let me trim them without violent resistance. He hissed at my friends. He routinely swatted at my beloved mother. He randomly bit when you pet him. He was patently untrainable. He was perfect. I had found my spirit animal, and he came in the form of a fascist cat.

In fact, he grew to act so notoriously dangerous towards the staff at the vet that we were kindly disinvited from ever coming back. Plus, they nominated us to be interviewed for Animal Planet's *My Cat From Hell*. Surprisingly, even though I submitted a 5-minute video of my girlfriend and I trimming his claws as he seamlessly screamed bloody murder at 120 decibels, we never got a callback. Luckily, I found a vet in town that exclusively serves cats, and Butters immediately made their "special needs" roster of patients who get sedated upon arrival. Even with sedation, he's been known to literally aggravate the shit out of himself and apparently all over the examination room– spirit animal, I tell you. (All apologies to the angelic staff of the Denver All Cat Clinic. You make my list of unsung heroes.)

And with my infatuation with this furry beast, the walls I had subconsciously erected around my feelings of emotional vulnerability slowly began to crumble. My hardened heart somehow softened. I started dating again. Instead of making excuses not to go to my friends' or sister's house for dinner, I found ways to make things happen. It didn't dawn on me at the time, but the emotional boost and reinvigoration for life that I received from adopting that kitty was no less than that which I initially received from going on anti-depressants in the wake of my father's suicide. Animals have always flipped my serotonin switch, but this little shit plumb crashed the system. Whatever designs depression had for staging a mutiny on my bounty were hissed, slashed, bit, and grifted upon by that finicky little kitty in a suave black suit. In no small measure, my life was on a dark trajectory, and I was spared this fate by a chance encounter with a famished kitten looking for a measly handout. We've been best friends ever since.

Greener Pastures

After almost four years in Clay's operation, logistical issues had more than run their course through the company. The retail stores were doing alright, but the soaring cost of cannabis had come back down to Earth after a few years of full legalization. Pounds of flower that used to go for over $3k per pound crumbled to less than half of that. More players were on the scene. More operations had survived the learning curve of the first few years of industry, and our competition's quality was beginning to approach that of our own. Our increasingly inefficient production facility was no longer keeping up with the market corrections, and upper management's hand was forced. Staying the course that got us to that point was no longer an option. Major moves had to be made to survive the bottleneck of those who would make it through the "tougher times." Little did we know then, but the actual "tougher times" were still years away– when prices would someday bottom out below the $500/lb. mark.

So, the company brass signed a deal with the devil disguised as venture capitalists. The roof of our current facility was slowly collapsing inwards– due to all of the added HVAC equipment required to transform an office into a cultivation facility. Every time it rained or the snow melted, the roof would leak in no less than a dozen different places scattered throughout the floorplan of the building. Once confined to only the walls, the black mold rapidly took up additional residence in the ceiling. Since we were renting the property, and we had effectively destroyed the infrastructure of the building to the point of it needing to be gutted down to the studs, we were forced to move our operation, and quickly. We were presented with the only game in town, so we signed.

Ultimately, we rented a 120,000-square-foot retrofit facility in Northglenn, about 20 minutes north of Denver. On the surface, it looked to be a massive upgrade over our original facility. Not only was it over 20 times the size, but it looked the part. The building had well over 2,200 double-ended, high-pressure-sodium lights, the more current technology than the less than 200 single-ended bulb units we were used to working with. The HVAC wasn't a hot mix of residential-grade units added on to the existing structure of the building– our disastrous approach to the first facility. No, this building had eight state-of-the-art cooling units, each roughly 20 feet high, 20 feet wide, and 15 feet deep. Each unit ranged from 100-160 tons of cooling capacity. In perspective, your average home's A/C ranges from 3-5 tons. The place was so gargantuan that the Marijuana Enforcement Division of Colorado (the official cannabis regulating body) informed us that the facility was easily one of the largest legal outfits in the state.

Instead of staying pat with our decaying Platte River facility trudging ever so closer to total catastrophic failure, upper management went for it and signed on to a massive lease, leaving us solely responsible for all upkeep and repairs. For the next ten years, we were committed. It was the only choice, and it was a choice that would upset the apple cart I had grown to love intimately.

We already had our routines. We knew the premises of the Platte facility and their functionality–or lack thereof– like perfect clockwork. Starting over in a new building on another side of town would be a monumental shift in that production paradigm I once knew. No longer the same 10:00 and 2:00 breaks to watch the River People. No more lackadaisical harvests, taking our sweet time to bitch and joke and jockey the playlist on the loudspeaker. Just like that, we had a deadline to keep our current facility baseline functional long enough to move operations across town successfully and not lose our genetic library of strains in the process.

As Clay's lead grower, I would be tasked with double duty. I'd start my mornings at Platte to get the other growers going on the day's tasks, and then I would commute to the new warehouse to tend to the few hundred plants we moved over there when we first took over the lease. At first, it was not just manageable but conspicuously easy and entertaining to no end. I was afforded some social time with my colleagues in the morning. Delegate the bitchwork. Crack a few jokes. Buzz across town. Then, I'd relish my personal time in the afternoons, the single soul toiling about in a warehouse the size of two Wal-Marts. I bought myself a Razor scooter and a portable boombox. I scooted around my private palace every afternoon with a leisurely two to three hours of labor to perform. When it was just me, that primarily vacant warehouse, and a few hundred veg plants roughly two feet tall, life briefly imitated perfection.

But plants grow. And plants multiply when you're instructed to clone them. And clones grow and require more care and more cloning as they advance in age. Operations ramped up at a parabolic rate. Two-hour projects became four-hour projects. Four-hour projects became ten. Even so, we didn't ramp up resources accordingly. After about two months in the new facility, I could no longer split my time between the two. The growers down at the Platte facility had to man it without me. More to the point, when they would finish their minimal requisites of daily tasks, Kerry would periodically break them off to send them my way. Even with supplemental help, what initially took me less than an afternoon to accomplish in the new facility quickly snowballed into 10 to 12-hour days. More plants. Larger plants. Healthier plants. More voracious plants. More demanding plants. My one-man dream job was no more. In two months, I came to assume the responsibilities of two diligent growers. I've always been of the mindset to work smarter, not harder. To keep up with the horticultural demands of our infantile facility, I would have to do both with the intensity of a man doused in napalm and set ablaze.

I appealed to Clay. I appealed to Chaz. I appealed to every manager in the company who had an open ear for me. There just weren't enough funds to bring on and train enough capable people in real-time so that I could get the personnel resources I needed to keep my weeks at 40 reasonable working hours. Unsolicitedly, I would overstay my required hours daily so that none of my efforts were squandered. Turning hundreds of plants into thousands of plants and doing so within the guidelines of best practices was what I was tasked to do. That their collective demand for pampered treatment far outweighed the standardized eight hours of my working day was of little consequence. I didn't put in that much effort ultimately to see it forsaken by my company's inability to give me the resources needed to make that many specimens thrive. Could I have walked out at 5:00 every night, whatever the case? I could have. But I didn't. I had too much pride. I was the primary caretaker for that warehouse, and those plants directly reflected my professional worth. Neglecting them as late in the game as it happened to be was not an option. I stuck it out until I could stick it out no longer.

It was sometime in late February 2017 that I decided I had enough of Skyward and its wayward planning for success. For over a month, Clay and Chaz knew exactly how overworked and above and beyond I had gone to get the warehouse up and running. They knew I was routinely hitting 50+ hour work weeks of my own volition to rise above the challenge. They knew I was a linchpin in their plan to transition between facilities, and whether they realized it or not, they could have done more to meet my all-consuming level of commitment. I was outworking my bosses (who were also investors), my colleagues, and pretty much anyone else I had seen go about their business in the company. I pushed myself to an unreasonable standard of commitment, and I was frankly unimpressed with almost everyone who couldn't match my intensity. I was great at my job, despite the fact I knew I had a way to go if I was ever to approach the echelon of Clay or Darren.

Nonetheless, I was well on my way, and my dedication to the cause was second to none. The management of Skyward didn't seem to notice that despite my transcendent efforts, the tide was starting to turn in the warehouse, and the plants' continued health solely depended on my digging deeper than those around me. I became indignant and put in two months' notice with Clay that he could either bring me in as a partner, give me an obscene raise, or watch me walk. Clay couldn't disagree with a word of my gripes. He recognized the shortcomings of his upper management team. He commended me for my stalwart efforts. Clay thanked me for my service and accepted my two months' notice to walk. By April, I was done with Skyward Farms.

Following my four-year grind to lead-grower status, I figured I had more than paid my dues to the industry, one still very much in its infancy. In all reality, I had worked intimately enough with Clay that I knew his system frontwards and back. The only aspects of his program I didn't wholly understand were the fine-tuned nuances of plant nutrition. Indeed, I had a solid concept of what to feed the plants and when to feed them. Though I didn't precisely know the "why." Why use this recipe at this stage of plant development and that recipe at another? It didn't seem to matter as long as I could replicate what I already knew. I had copied a handful of varied recipes from Clay's repertoire and would simply take them with me whenever it was time for me to go and do my own thing. Aside from that, I knew how to run a reasonably sized facility. Maybe I wasn't a fully accomplished grower, but I was far more professional, driven, and obsessive than my pot-growing peers. For an industry as slapdash and fledgling as that, I seized my opportunity, maxed out my education under my predecessor, and took my talents to the open market.

Needless to say, I didn't immediately step away from Skyward and have a turnkey opportunity waiting for me on Day One. The first month or two of unemployment lent itself to the cliche Hollywood sound effect of crickets chirping in an empty room. My résumé was polished. It was relatively impressive. Recruiters and various HR managers told me as much. I had been a player in the industry for over half its existence, and my former boss was nationally known and respected within the community. I was his guy and had glowing recommendations to attach to my track record. However, finding the right opportunity to take over a suitable operation was much more tedious than I had originally anticipated.

The first position I interviewed for was so pathetic that I walked out halfway through when the GM went to the bathroom and didn't return for at least a half hour. The place was an unfixable disaster. The lights were wrong. The HVAC was wrong. The plants were puny and diseased. They had a rampant infestation of just about every pest in the book. The main flowering room had a hole in the ceiling measuring no less than 20 square feet. It made the Platte facility look like the Taj Mahal. Plus, they didn't want to fire their current leader. They wanted me to come in and collaborate with him. He was the owner's kid brother, so he wasn't going anywhere on principle. It was the equivalent of asking a four-star chef to work with the operator of a hotdog cart and concoct something from his unit that might take home a Michelin star. That was conclusively not the landing spot.

A few weeks later, I interviewed in Fort Morgan, Colorado. Unlike most of what I had seen in the Greater Denver area, this facility looked as though it was actually built to serve its intended purpose. It was about the same size as what I was used to at Platte, and it wasn't a complete tear-down. The rooms were built to specs. Each one had floor drains and sufficient environmental controls. The plants didn't look great, but after asking no more than five questions, I realized the fix was obvious. Their acting grower looked like a deer in headlights when I asked him what kinds of beneficial microbes he was adding to his soil bases. He had no idea that microbes were even a factor in horticulture. This is like being a doctor and not knowing the benefits of washing your hands. The place was being run by some naturalist stoner who looked the part but knew less regarding cultivation than your average cannabis consumer, much less producer.

It felt like a shoo-in. I met the owner, and he seemed like a solid guy. The GM was very likable and appeared to offer substantial support resources. He and I hit it off when we got to talking college football and the sad state of the Huskers. There were only two assistant growers to manage, and they purportedly had a reputation for dutifully managing themselves. The opportunity was brilliant, except that it was in Ft. Morgan. Lying about a hundred miles east of Denver, it is unfortunately out of sight of the Rocky Mountains. I'm no psychoanalyst, but for whatever reason, as soon as I lose sight of those mountains on the horizon, things mysteriously get sullen in my world. For all practical purposes, if I look west and can't see the Rockies, I might as well be standing in Nebraska or Kansas.

Rather than outright turn down the job because of the geographical happenstance, I subconsciously self-sabotaged and presented them with a take-it-or-leave-it opportunity to pay me well above market value to relocate to such a place. Thankfully, I did. It was enough to price myself out of contention. I'm reasonably confident I could have taken that position if I let it come to me, but whether I was conscious of it or not, no amount of money would have made that move worthwhile. Unfortunately, due to the curvature of the Earth and the limits of human vision, the opportunity resided just outside of my natural element, and some things just can't be compensated for by monetary means.

In full accordance with the universal motif of "three being the magic number," I discovered my next destination upon my third interview. I found myself almost four months removed from Skyward– about twice as long as I would have initially anticipated– and more than anything, I just wanted to get back to work. As it would turn out, I interviewed with a couple of former Major League Baseball players, and I hit it off with them from the first introductions. They explicitly appreciated my forthrightness and that I disclaimed from the outset that I was no expert in horticultural affairs. I explained my professional history, how I learned what I professed to know, and my commitment to continuously developing my craft. I knew I was far from being what many in the industry commonly refer to as a "master grower," and I insisted they understood that I was a curated work in progress.

I'm not sure master growers even exist insofar as anyone with that level of understanding of plant life would almost certainly denounce such titles. Plant life is life, and life is not wholly comprehensible from the human perspective. The most enlightened of botanists would never presume to understand conclusively the phenomena of cannabis cultivation, and I knew I wasn't even marginally of their standing. I was a liberal arts major, turned high-end customer service widget, and spent the past four years learning a new industry from the soil upwards. I happened to cut my teeth under a renowned operator in Clay, and I leveraged my standing as his protégé to establish credibility by proxy. I knew a lot, and what I didn't know, I professed to actively seek out and learn. My Skyward credentials and my overly pronounced projection of humility were enough to convince them I was worth giving a shot as chief operator of their cultivation down in Trinidad– not Trinidad as in Tobago, but Trinidad as in 14 miles north of the New Mexico border on I-25.

Albeit a tempting offer, it had its obvious drawbacks, the foremost being that it was located over three hours away. It was still Colorado, an unnegotiable, overriding detail learned organically from my time waffling around California. It was nestled at the Rockies' foothills, satisfying my quizzical prerequisite for geographical, long-term livability. It was even a touch bigger in population than Aspen, a community just large enough to provide all of the rudimentary comforts of multiple grocery stores and restaurants– enticing women folk, not so much.

Even so, it was not Denver. My sister and my friends would be a road trip away, and if I were to jump into what was being proposed, I would have virtually no time to make that trip. I loved Denver but was growing tired of living in the pandemonium of the Capitol Hill area. I had shortsightedly put a time constraint on my job search by walking away from Skyward without a plan, and my options to date were far fewer than I had anticipated. Whatever designs I had on procuring an ideal opportunity for myself briskly reconfigured to me finding any opportunity, so long as I would be in charge of the daily growing operations.

I accepted their offer. I would pack up my apartment of almost six years, load a U-Haul, and become the Director of Cultivation for Higher Education Cannabis Company, an outfit located only in Trinidad and owned by two former MLB teammates, Clark Pendergrass and Buck Hayes, of the St. Louis Cardinals. Don't bother Googling them. You won't find anything under either of those names nor in the annals of Cardinals baseball history. As a friendly reminder from the introduction, some aspects of this memoir had to be modified to preserve everyone's privacy. Just know that their status as professional athletes prevailed as the ultimate factor, the superficial razzle-dazzle that would solidify my decision to accept the offer. My inner sports geek proved itself my Achilles.

Clark was the alpha of the two. Once an All-American pitcher for an SEC blueblood and resultant second-round draft pick to the Cardinals in the late '80s, his career would be cut tragically short by Tommy John surgery performed between his first and second year in the League. He got called up from AAA in late August of his rookie season, and by mid-September, he had torn the UCL in the elbow of his right (throwing) arm. He never recovered his fastball or command of the strike zone after the surgery and was labeled a "flop" when he found himself out of baseball by age 24. To his credit, Clark knew that baseball was just baseball and that his self-worth wasn't predicated on the op-ed column from some 1985 edition of *Sports Illustrated*. He was a scrapper. He held numerous occupations and titles over the years. He had been mildly successful in a few of his enterprises, and Higher Education was his American Dream. Clark liquidated one of his more successful operations in the car wash industry in order to raise sufficient capital to buy his way into the Trinidad cannabis market.

Clark was charming and handsome and knew how to work a room. He was polished and deliberate. Whether commiserating with the budtenders in the store or negotiating pricing with our carbon dioxide vendor, he could make someone feel remarkably unique if he felt like making an effort. When I was offered the opportunity to relocate to Trinidad, Clark had done his magic. He made me feel special enough to believe this was all in divine ordination. This man was a stud, and I thought myself to be of the same ilk. No, I wasn't, nor have I ever been the swarthy 6'3" hulk that Clark was. But I knew my place in the game, and with Clay's tutelage as my street credit, I felt myself to be of a distinction worthy enough to serve my larger-than-life boss.

Plus, Clark was only half of the appeal. Buck Hayes was a gem of a soul. Buck's story is that he was a longtime journeyman left-fielder for over a decade. Buck and Clark met at Buck's last stop in St. Louis. Leading up to that, Buck played for the Expos, Orioles, Brewers, Angels, and Astros. Originally hailing from a South Dakota farm just two miles from the Canadian border, Buck was as authentic and grounded as any professional athlete on this planet could possibly be. Forever the preacher's son that he was, Buck's preoccupation was far more centered around the happiness of his employees than his company's bottom line. Buck didn't live in town, but when he would stay on one of his extended visits, every day, he would deliver donuts to his people in the retail store and the production facility. He actively inquired with each of us, ensuring we had everything we needed to do our jobs and enjoy ourselves as we went about our business. His only drawback was that he wasn't intellectually sharp.

He might have been at one point, but in his last year in the League, he took a high heater squarely to the side of his batting helmet and was knocked unconscious for quite some time. According to Clark, Buck's mental capacities slowed dramatically after the incident. After that game, Buck would never play again, never live without some measure of a headache, and would see his cognitive abilities of memory and math skills regress to those of a flustered child. Buck loved to opine on this policy or that practice, but as Clark once secretively informed me, despite their supposed 50/50 partnership, Buck had no operational pull. Due to the injury that took him from the game, Clark insisted that Buck was more of the company's mascot than half the brass of Higher Ed. Let him verbally spin his wheels all he wanted to on me. I just had to smile and nod. I didn't care either way. As long as Buck was happy and placated, and I diligently followed Clark's lead, all else could be improvised as we went. They were cool guys and presented me with an opportunity I had dreamed about for quite some time.

My directive was cut and dry. Clark needed to fire his current grower and the grower's support staff and have me step in with my team, ready to take over and rehabilitate what had become sheer disarray of an operation. Curtis, the current grower, was infamous in town— as was advertised in my interview and was confirmed in the subsequent weeks by numerous townies— for treating people, namely his workers, like inhuman garbage. His flowers were known for mediocre quality, and his average weights per harvest were unconvincing at best to Clark and Buck. Even the folksy, downhome electrician, when I met him, went out of his way to remark on how much "Curtis was a no-good, son of a bitch." The bar couldn't have gone much lower.

All I had to do was devise a roster of four or five respectable growers and customize the tenets of Clay's system for this unique operation, though one of similar size and demand as that of Skyward's Platte facility. It was a scale I could more than handle. Plus, the building wasn't a retrofit. It was appropriately sized and outfitted with environmental controls I had yet to enjoy. Floor drains and ample dehumidification in each room were every bit as integral as I'd imagined they'd be. The veg rooms were outfitted with L.E.D. lights, a far superior and more forgiving technology than anything I was previously privileged to then. The genetic library was twice as manageable as Skyward's, considering it was less than half its size in variation. The quality of that stock was proven and ready for the commandeering. I wouldn't be expected to spend months testing one strain against the next, surveying the economic viability of each individualized phenotype– the necessary best-practices inventory taken when a grower assumes control over a new library. It seemed as plug-and-play as humanly possible.

My biggest obstacle in relocating to Trinidad was the housing factor. Through my research, I found no more than three apartment complexes in town that weren't of the Section-8 variety. Only one had a garish 3-bedroom vacancy, 30 years past its prime. The carpets were a gridded matrix of threadbare foot traffic patterns. Tributaries of cracks converged into rivers of grime running the length of the off-pink, formica kitchen countertops. It was just a notch above being a fully-fledged shithole. It was also the best of three total offerings in town. The other two were houses twice as expensive, and each looked like a murder house, one from the '50s and the other from the '70s.

My apartment was the nicest of the group, and after living in an off-interstate motel room for almost a week with my restless cat, I had to park it somewhere. I signed a month-to-month lease, and Butters and I were home. Trinidad, Colorado, was where we would make our stand. The professional success I had never imagined possible for myself during my years waiting tables was tantalizingly close to fruition. I would undeniably be well on my way to vocational prosperity in a few short weeks.

Omens and Outbreaks

Trinidad, Colorado– where to begin? As I was informed by the maintenance man of the apartment complex, Trinidad was a cultural enigma unlike most any other I had likely encountered in my 35 years. It was established in the 1860s as a coal mining town on the eastern edge of the legendary Wild West. Once a hideout for Billy the Kid on the lam, Trinidad has traditionally been a community that has been no stranger to flouting the law. After subsequently suffering over a century of boom/bust economy– based on the purportedly volatile nature of the coal mining industry– the once-proud, working-class narrative of the townsfolk progressively took on a defeatist attitude. Generations of families learned to live lean, take whatever they could get for work, and rely on government help to bridge the gaps.

Being the closest Colorado town to the state's southern border, it seized its opportunity in the mid-2010s to once again boom and tether its economy to the insatiable black market demands of its prohibitionist neighbors of New Mexico and Texas. In 2017, at any time and on any day, over half of the license plates on the roads of Trinidad sported a license plate of one of those two states. For a town of 7,000 inhabitants, 23 dispensaries glared as gluttonous overkill. It was a smuggler's town, and everyone knew it. In lockstep with its polarized past, Trinidad found itself awash in an embarrassment of excess. It had too many producers, too many retailers, too many smugglers, too many people up to nefarious things. After welcoming me to my humblest of abodes, teaching me the town's tragic history, and advising me to get a home security system– as a rash of midday break-ins had recently overtaken the community– my local, friendly maintenance man wished me best in my endeavor to field a functional team of cannabis pros. His parting giggle as he left my unit couldn't have been more ominous.

In addition to myself, Clark also simultaneously recruited a Post-Harvest/Compliance Manager from Denver, a guy named Kenny

Cartwright. Kenny and I were tasked with overhauling the warehouse staff. I was charged with finding growers. Kenny had to assess what he wanted to do with the trimming staff. As a matter of principle, once the head of a cultivation department is fired, it's considered prudent to relinquish as many of his loyal disciples as you can logistically manage. "Sabotage" is a term that has unfortunately grown to become synonymous with spurned cannabis cultivators, and throwing a horticultural operation into an irreparable tailspin is something all too easy for even a total imbecile to actualize. A scorned, petty grower left in the garden is an open-ended liability no operator should ever entertain. The existing grow team, led by Curtis, couldn't be tipped off to our secretive recruitment of their replacements. No classifieds for the new team were run in the region. Nobody outside of Clark, Buck, Kenny, and myself had any idea that monumental changes were strategically being undertaken within the operations of Higher Education.

After our communal deliberation on the matter, it was decided that because the four full-time trimmers we employed had a track record for consistently diligent working practices and because Curtis had treated them like such expendable commodities– hence, their exacted disdain for his previous regime– that they would pose no risk if they were to be retained. Within the warehouse, he had effectively designated them second-class citizens. They never received their two legally-mandated 15-minute breaks during their days. They were expected to work in silence. Talking, laughing, and camaraderie were expressly forbidden during working hours. They weren't allowed to view any living plants, much less lend helping hands in communal cultivation processes. He didn't ask about their families. From what I understand, he didn't even bother using their names. Every trimmer was unilaterally lumped into a homogenized, fourth-person typecast of "you." They had no allegiance to their former boss and openly celebrated his demise and our arrival on Day One. They could stay.

The growers, on the other hand, positively had to go. Based on what Clark and Buck explained to Kenny and me as we plotted our swift takeover, the grow team had an almost cultlike allegiance to Curtis. They were all of his buddies, and due to the incestuous nature of mixing business with intimate friendships, the culture in the cultivation took on a carte blanche disposition. Upper management had no say if Kenny arbitrarily wanted something done this way or that. He simply did it, and his minions unquestioningly complied. He became his own little Jim Jones of a Tier-1 cannabis cultivation, and the bosses were having none of it. Not only was he ubiquitously known throughout town as a wretch, but he had no problem dictating to the powers that be. Instead of working proactively with the retail GM or taking the simplest of directions from the company's owners, he effectively challenged them to try and replace him.

And that's precisely what we aimed to do. I was brought to town on a Sunday to spend a week living out of a motel, parsing through accrued résumés, and scheduling interviews with potential growers, all while doing so as secretively as possible. Trinidad was too small, and one loose-lipped applicant could blow our meticulously devised cover. If word was to get out to Curtis or any of his loyalists, irrefutably, they were of a reputation that would rather see that operation burn to the ground before being handed over like gentlemanly scholars. To call it a unique overhaul of one's support staff would be a gross understatement. If we were to get this right, we had to be religiously cautious with our every word. By Saturday, I silently needed to find four to five serviceable laborers and ones with enough common sense not to blow the lid on our cunning takeover of the production facility. This convergence of circumstances would afford us less than a week to preserve our secret of paramount importance.

Over that first week of clandestine interviewing processes, I came to two monumental realizations. The first was that the professional talent pool in Trinidad was so underwhelming that any pretenses I had of plugging and playing any given applicant into my system would be incredibly far-fetched. The stack of résumés I was initially handed was a veritable cornucopia of laughs. Most were printed uniformly in standard, 12-pt., double-spaced, Times New Roman font. Most listed a name, phone number, address (as though I might correspond with them via USPS), and one or two personal references. Maybe half of them had one to three entries regarding prior employment. Half of those didn't even offer contact information for their professional superiors. One résumé I looked at was eight pages long, printed on a dot-matrix printer, contained maybe four points of data pertinent enough to be included on a list of credentials, and boasted a series of pixellated pictures of the applicant posing with a hoe in one hand and a shovel in the other– all in front of plants that resembled nothing of cannabis. How did I know it was dot-matrix material? It was one seamless ream of perforated paper, fully intact, and accordioned into something that came at you like a jack-in-the-box. This exposé conducted among thistle bushes in a vacant construction lot had all the touches of a *GQ* photoshoot.

The second realization I made was that if I were to have a prayer at getting this thing off the ground, it would require at least two months of unimaginable effort. Of the approximately 20 résumés I was initially handed, only seven or eight qualified for realistic consideration. I needed over half of that pool to hit if this was going to work. Even if half of them did hit, I knew there was no way that they would all be trained enough for me to enjoy any of my days off without worrying that everything would irretrievably fall into disarray in my absence. The art of curating a successful plant cycle takes weeks and months of diligence to get right. Yet, only a fleeting moment of environmental chaos can nullify all of that exertion in a heartbeat. An operation is only as effective as its worst grower, so making one lousy hire could make it all for naught. I critically needed to get things right.

With that, I made my selections. The first guy I hired interviewed the best of the bunch. His name was Daryl. At first sight, you could tell that he was a character hailing from a latchkey background. The prison tattoo of a teardrop on his cheek was his first talking point. Rather than let me speculate one way or another on that universal indicator of former incarceration, he brought to my attention that he was an individual who used to run with the wrong crowd, made some bad decisions regarding the drugs he decided to rely on for coping strategies, and that his time served achieved its ideological purpose. Daryl proclaimed himself a new man, looking for a better way to live out his days. In conjunction with his non-laughable résumé and blue-collar attitude toward wanting to work himself ragged, his forthrightness in taking restorative agency over his life won me over. I had no choice but to offer him the job as a grower. With discernable delight, he accepted on the spot. One-for-one wasn't a bad batting average for someone making their first-lifetime professional hire. The next few weren't entirely as straightforward.

On paper, I was reluctant to call Jeremy in for an interview. His résumé might even have been the last to make the cut, mainly because the one featured position he had listed was that of a Wal-Mart "cart pusher." Trying not to sound too presumptuous, I can only say that seeing an official title listed as such on a résumé did not induce the most promising of premonitions. That it didn't dawn on this Jeremy character that "parking lot attendant" or "logistics associate" might read a hundred times more respectably to a potential employer than "cart pusher" was almost sad. Had the pickings not been as tragically slim as they were, I wouldn't have bothered to call him in. As it turned out, Jeremy ironically became one of my most dependable growers. He was a tick over five-foot tall, sweet as a hospice nurse, and never looked at the clock during the workday. He could plug away for eight hours straight, and he might sheepishly request one quick piss break. He was the sleeper of the bunch– the all-star proletariat surreptitiously disguised as a hapless "cart pusher."

The following two hires were a package deal: two cousins who did everything together, Bartolo and Julio. Wherever one spent his days, the other was in a stone's throw proximity. Wherever one worked, the other typically worked. When Julio interviewed and impressed me with the rarity of his associate's degree from Trinidad Junior College, I had no choice but to take his word that his cousin was equally as genuine as he was. After them, I was down to two more résumés in the pile, and neither of them exactly screamed as being a slam dunk. Julio and his purportedly steadfast cousin would have to suffice. I had maybe two days left before the big takeover, and when it came to labor, even warm bodies were better than no bodies.

The last two résumés of the pile were indeed nothing more than ornamental. One person had no intention of accepting any employment. I'm guessing they were simply working the unemployment system, handing out the requisite three to five résumés weekly to maintain their benefits. The other applicant had already worked for the company during the era of Curtis' predecessor and had been fired for stealing buds from the plants. That he had the gall to walk back into the dispensary a few years later and leave his contact info for future openings is truly a testament to the deluded ethos of the local employment pool.

The last grower to make the roster was a lady named Veronica. Fortuitously, we discovered her as she was married to one of the dispensary managers. She wasn't actively looking for employment but was happy to get an unsolicited opportunity thrown her way. Incidentally, her résumé trumped all the others. She spent over five years in the Navy as an intelligence officer stationed in various locations throughout the Middle East. She was sharp, humble, eager to learn, and followed directions like no other person I had ever met in that industry. Her husband, Ryan, was considered a bit of a loose cannon in the dispensary. He was brazen and often grumpy. He didn't smile a whole lot nor exude any outward positivity toward the clientele. Nonetheless, he was more than employable by Trinidad standards and was fun to hang out with off of the clock. Despite his gruff nature, people seemed to naturally like him, myself very much included.

My team was set. With just over a day left before the takeover, I had found five promising applicants in what would otherwise be considered the bottom of the barrel in almost any other market in the cannabis-producing United States. The lot of them were generally likable. Each professed to want to learn the system I appropriated from Clay. They all appeared to be the obvious selections from my limited supply of applicants, and none of them felt like a reach. Even in Denver, all five hires would have been regarded as legitimate prospects for long-term employment. That was the last time I would harbor such unwarranted optimism towards the team in its entirety.

What auspiciously began as a most fortunate hiring cycle was immediately compromised by my first hire, Daryl. With each of the five hires, I made the situation with the current production staff *explicitly and abundantly* clear. All of the interviews were being conducted in secrecy, and anyone who would accept an offered position *absolutely, positively must not* spill the beans on what Clark, Buck, Kenny, and I had so meticulously orchestrated. All they had to do was show up at the production facility at 9 AM on Saturday, and a new era of life would begin for us all. That was too complicated for Daryl.

On Friday morning, around 9:10, I received a phone call from him saying that he showed up at the facility, knocked on the door, and told whoever answered the door that he was there for his first day of work with the new Director of Cultivation. He was confused when no one at the facility had any idea what he was referring to. Just like that, our best-laid plans were toast. Curtis and his sordid coalition of miscreants were granted roughly two hours of unfettered access to a production facility from which they knew they would be momentarily fired.

As soon as Daryl inadvertently admitted his transgression to me, I called an emergency meeting with Kenny and the bosses, and we scrambled to pull the plug on Curtis and his team's access to the facility. We frantically improvised, and by noon, we flipped the personnel in the warehouse. It wouldn't be another week or two until I realized it, but the damage was already done in those two hours. Unbeknownst to any of us, as we learned a few months after, when those guys got wind they were going to be replaced, they reached out to colleagues at competing facilities in search of spider mite infestations. They actively shopped around town for the notoriously stalwart, voracious pests.

As rumor would have it, immediately after getting fired, the bunch of them went to their local dive bar of choice and celebrated a sabotage "that new guy would never have the ability to overcome." As it would turn out, they weren't wrong. By my second week in charge of the facility, at least half of the eight flowering rooms were infested with spider mites to a degree that I had only seen in photos. A few bugs here and there are par for the course in almost all commercial operations. This was more than a few bugs. Before we even had a chance to realize there was a problem, it was too late. Each room boasted at least a half-dozen plants with circus tent-like webbing enshrouding each from the top cola clear down to the soil line. If it wasn't my problem and it wasn't a completely dickless, underhanded thing to do, I might have even applauded their efforts. In less than two hours, they prolifically exacted revenge on a person they previously never even knew existed. This was the culture I was charged to reform.

Day One was every bit as chaotic as I anticipated it would be. We just fired an entire grow staff. Curtis had forcefully kept the trimmers we retained in an informational bubble, so unfortunately, they didn't have any shortcut answers for where this might be located or where that should go. I had five strangers to drown in a crash course of both plant theory and standard operating procedures. I had survived several professional baptisms by fire, but no amount of preparation whatsoever could have properly readied me to navigate those waters gracefully. If I even had one assistant steeped in Clay's system, the transition would have gone nothing short of 400% less aggravating than was the case. As reality would have it, I spent an inordinate amount of the day showing grown adults how to move 55-gallon drums of feedwater around the building without spilling them or ramming holes into the walls' baseboards with the transport dollies. Common sense was at a premium. Had it not been for the militaristic capabilities of Veronica babysitting the boys, I'm not entirely sure I wouldn't have rethought my entire professional trajectory on the spot. She wasn't a member of Mensa, but compared to the rest of the team, she might as well have held tenure at Princeton. By day's end, she was publicly deemed my right-hand lady. If I was out of the room, Veronica was in charge– no questions asked.

Day Two was even more memorable than day one. Operationally speaking, things were 2000% more productive. With a learning curve from the previous day as brutal as it was, an astronomical leap forward was our only option. Even so, a turd is a turd, and the monumental uphill ascent in getting those boys up to functional speed required Veronica and me to exercise our inner Kindergarten teachers to bridge the gap in real-time. Plants were aplenty, and just because the company made massive overhauls in policy, the cannabis couldn't have cared less. Much like the operational setup of Skyward, this place was on a strict eight-week schedule of repetition, and we were already a few days behind the eightball as far as the plants were concerned. Based on how neglected the plant stock had visibly become under Curtis' lackadaisical watch, those first two days were indeed us racing the clock. Despite our frenetic triage to save what biomass we could, what vividly demarcates day two from every other day I spent in Trinidad had nothing to do with horticulture.

At some point in the late morning, when we got to a point where all of the morning rooms (those with the grow lights on until noon) were watered, all of us reconvened in the garage to break up bales of soil and prefill pots for transplants later in the day. About five minutes into the laborious task, Daryl must have overheated as he stopped to take off his sweatshirt. Not a second after casting the article of clothing aside, I noticed the thematic tattoos strewn conspicuously up and down each arm. Much like the movie trope where the character makes a paramount realization and the room suddenly fades out of focus, all sound mutes to zero, and in slow-motion, they shrink away in disbelief, I nearly collapsed when all the blood drained from my extremities.

"Seig Heil," "White Power," "Mein Kampf," "Aryan Brotherhood," and "New World Order" were surprisingly some of the more civil declarations. Prison-quality sketches of knives, guns, bats, pools of blood, lifeless bodies, and a full-tricep rendition of a commemorative Panzer tank with the initials A.H. and the years 1889-1945 emblazoned across the side– those tattoos must've glowed red in the dark. The raging hate they conveyed hit me with a force I had never experienced before nor since. It's not as if I grew up in a bubble where anti-semitism was a legend of the antiquated past. Growing up, I'd encountered my share of latent bigotry aimed against Jews. Perhaps it was a swastika carved into a bench or the lazy cliche joke of getting "Jewed" out of a couple of dollars. As alienating as those things may have been, they were Kumbaya, We-Are-The-World stuff compared to what Daryl had scrawled across his flesh. The most physically revolting of them all was a noose encircling a word I subsequently had to look up on Urban Dictionary later in the day. I'm proud to declare I previously had no idea it was an epithet pertaining to African Americans. Suffice it to say, I quickly exited the room, equally as nauseous as I was speechless.

There is no word to describe my sensation upon entering the hallway. Here I was– a card-carrying, circumcized, Bar Mitzvahed, rabbi's younger brother– and I accidentally hired myself a shit-sucking, sister-fucking Nazi. He interviewed in long sleeves. He grew out his hair. He disclaimed his teardrop tattoo with a rehearsed backstory any person with one iota of grace and forgiveness would have bought in full. I made five hires to help me actualize my ambitious endeavor, and 20% of them most likely wished me dead. The best thing I had going for me was that he wasn't too bright, and neither my last name nor my plainly Jewish face was enough to set off his Jewdar. Who would have thought a bona fide racist wouldn't have the intellectual capacity to demonstrate the profiling skills of an educated sixth-grader?

I immediately dialed up Clark. I recall almost hyperventilating as I explained the situation and the fact that there was no dimension of the universe where Daryl stayed employed by Higher Ed, and I remained his boss. Clearly, I had unknowingly made a deal-breaker of a hire in bringing on Daryl, but we had to part ways with him. Either Clark could cut him loose, or I could go back to my schleppy apartment, pack it up in two hours, eat the loss of the rest of the month's rent, and he could hire someone else to take things over. Admittedly, it was a bit of an unfair demand to drop on my new boss, seeing as how I made the hire, and I was the one unable to proceed forward as such.

Nonetheless, I was Heinlein's "stranger in a strange land," with no friends, allies, or securities of any sort. Clark was a physically imposing former professional athlete, and as coward-like as it might have been, I was not willing to become the crosstown-Kike that hired and fired and added to Daryl's narrative of his white man's burden. In light of my maintenance man's forewarning, I found myself compulsively envisioning the morbidity of coming home one day from my gainful employment to find a ransacked apartment and a crucified cat. I'll be honest. Despite Clark gifting me the major solid of doing my dirty work for me, I was quietly terrified for a few weeks after the fact. I had no idea how broken of a person Daryl may or may not have been, nor what he might be capable of doing to someone like me in a place where anonymity simply didn't exist. Luckily, after that, I only saw him twice out and about town, and neither time did he seem to notice me.

I firmly believe that things transpire as they should and that fixating on notions of having done things differently to change the past is the stuff of make-believe. What's done is done, and there's no sense squandering two seconds deliberating the hypothetical alternatives. Even so, with the gift of hindsight, I'll go ahead and say the Daryl situation should have been a glaring harbinger of things to come my way in the next eight months.

On the plus side, my presence at that time was integrated and forceful enough to bulldoze the prevailing stratification of the fundamentally toxic working culture Curtis had left behind. More than my drive to impress my bosses with larger, healthier, and more profitable plants, I was determined to make every last person in the facility feel like they were seen and heard as people, not widgets. Upon taking over my position, hearing the plight of the trimmers was more than enough to upset me to action. On principle, they would take their breaks with the rest of us, learn and interact with the system of live-plant cultivation, get respectable discounts in the retail shop (seeing as how they previously couldn't even afford to sample their own work), and be seen and heard as men. Naturally, my hired staff–Nazis notwithstanding– were also trained to be assertive in lobbying for their most optimal working conditions. No, I couldn't indulge everyone's every request. Nonetheless, I empowered them to view themselves as more than just employees of someplace they had to go daily to pay the man. With zero speculation to the contrary, this was decidedly my most notable (perhaps only) achievement from my time in Trinidad.

Conversely, I was never able to right the ship the way I had so righteously intended. And it wasn't for a lack of effort. For eight months, I averaged 55-hour work weeks. I went over three weeks on end with no days off on numerous occasions. I sweat. I bled. I cried my ass off more than once.

Despite the most consummate effort I had ever expended on *any* undertaking I had ever made in my 35 years, I just couldn't get things over the hump. The expenses I was incurring from running Clay's bells-and-whistles nutrient regimen weren't even close to offsetting the fact that I had yet to improve the per-harvest average of yields by the pound. It didn't matter that the quality of my final product compared to that of Curtis was night and day. The fact of the matter was that I couldn't for my life figure out how to implement an entirely predictable, scalable process for harvesting more than 25 pounds of dope weekly. I was given the option to amend the nutrient recipes drastically, but I didn't know how. When I admitted that to my bosses– a reminder from my initial interview that I still had a ways to go in understanding plant nutrition– my fate was sealed. Two days later, Clark unceremoniously called me into the manager's office to shake my hand and wish me well on my way.

I had failed. It was only the second time in my life I had been fired from a job, and even though I had grown to realize I was not the man for this particular overhaul, it crushed me that I had been let go. Exactly one year earlier, I had walked from Skyward, dead certain that I had all of the requisite skills to run my own operation, yet low and behold, I hadn't. Was I far off? Not at all. Before I was canned, we had a consultant come in, and he came to find that my singular problem was that the soil bases of the plants were getting "hot," thereby stunting the root growth, nutrient uptake, and, ultimately, harvest weights. Despite my training the growers to water each room to the point that 10-15% of the volume of liquid feed runs out the bottom of the plants, they hadn't followed that protocol as regularly as necessary. This resulted in a massive buildup of unconsumed salts accruing at the bottom of each pot– a condition detrimental to optimal growth.

By the time we became aware of this highly curable issue, I had already sealed my fate with Clark. After eight months of living in relative isolation from my friends and family and after having run myself straight into the ground with my masochistic working efforts, it had become a well-known fact within the company that I was non-too-impressed with what had become of my life in Trinidad. I legitimately liked and respected no more than a half-dozen people in town, and fewer people than that were likely to return the sentiment.

I had run through almost ten growers by the time Clark decided. Jeremy was the only one who went the distance with me. Unfortunately, because Veronica's husband, Ryan, got caught stealing from the store, he was immediately terminated, and she had to go based on association. I wasn't even given a choice. He was gone, so she had to follow. The other guys fizzled out like teenagers working summer jobs. No matter the consequences, 9 AM start times often faded into 9:15, 9:30, or just before noon. One dingus even called me one morning an hour after the fact to tell me that his son wanted to watch the Halloween parade in town, so he would consequently be at work sometime after lunch.

When I relayed to ownership the reality of how patently unreliable my staff had become, I was met with disinterested recognition– tough shit for me. If one of my guys didn't feel like showing up for the weekend shift, it was my problem and mine alone. Those three-week benders of me trudging through 10 to 12-hour days broke me in the end. I couldn't remedy the local talent pool, and after months and months of fighting the malaise of the prevailing local work ethic, I was systematically disenchanted to the depths of perfect apathy. Having invested as much as I did in my endeavors, there was no way in hell I was ever going to quit. No matter how miserable and disenfranchised life had become, Clark *had* to fire me to separate me from the opportunity. There was no alternative.

For maybe an hour after the dismissal, I languished in a space of "What happened, and how could I have done things differently?" Aside from failing to stress to my subordinates the importance of water runoff, there wasn't a whole lot else I did incorrectly. I planned, plodded, and executed with every last faculty of my body and mind. It didn't work, and thank God Clark ripped off the band-aid for the both of us.

Every last facet of my existence in Trinidad was forced, fruitless, and evermore noxious with each day that tediously slogged by. I had uprooted my existence from a place I loved immeasurably and relocated to a jurisdiction within Colorado that proved far more alien to me than any other locale I have since discovered in the state. I sacrificed leisure time and quality time with my loved ones. I gained almost 30 pounds by quitting all forms of exercise– as a matter of timely necessity– and by subsisting on a diet of fast food and frozen pizza. The one person I had grown friendly enough to hang out with regularly, Kenny, quit speaking with me as soon as Clark made it official that I was gone and that Kenny would be the interim D.O.C. until they could find my suitable replacement– their sixth department head in four years.

Within 72 hours of dismissal, my U-haul was packed. Just like that, my time in the diaspora had ended. I came. I tried. I failed. I was graciously cast back into the ether.

With Butters at my side, the two of us hit the I-25 offramp North, and back in Denver, our story would continue. With my only true Trinidad companion at my side, I glued the pedal to the floor and belted out a triumphant "Yeeeehawwwww!' The anguish of Trinidad had ended.

Whimsically, we sped our way back home.

161

[*To Be Continued...*]

About the Author

Zachary Perelman is a reformed asshole, an existentialist, and a Legacy Doula based in Denver, Colorado. His overriding preoccupation in life is helping individuals discover their unique, intrinsic values and how to best endow their legacies to the world at large. In addition to the aspect of legacy work, he focuses his efforts on the aging, elderly, and/ or dying demographic of humanity. His mission is to inject that space with as much dignity, compassion, comfort, peace, and meaning as one can possibly receive while transitioning from this earthly life. It took over four decades to come to the realization, but ultimately, he found his purpose in the service of others.

Read more at yourtimelesstravels.com.